I0115636

The Orchestration of the Failure of Society

An Updated Independent Companion & Addendum to the
volume entitled *Seven Men Who Rule the World from the Grave*
by Dave Breese

By:

Jason Randolph

The Orchestration of the Failure of Society

An Updated Independent Companion & Addendum to the
volume entitled
Seven Men Who Rule the World from the Grave by Dave
Breese

By:

Jason Randolph

Copyright ©2014, Clerestory Books, an imprint of
Shelf*Bloom ePress | JASON RANDOLPH

All rights reserved. No part of this publication may be
reproduced, distributed, or transmitted in any form or by any
means, including photocopying, recording, or other electronic or
mechanical methods, without the prior written permission of the
publisher, except in the case of brief quotations embodied in
critical reviews, church/Bible study presentations and certain
other noncommercial uses permitted by copyright law. For

permission requests, write to the publisher, addressed "Attention: Permissions" at the address below.

Clerestory Books
PO BOX 1104
Langlois, Oregon 97450

Ordering Information:

Quantity sales. Special discounts are available on quantity purchases by corporations, associations, and others. For details, contact the publisher at the address above.

Orders by U.S. trade bookstores and wholesalers. Please contact Shelf*Bloom ePress: Tel: (888) 632-6762; or visit http://c.shelfbloom.com.

ISBN 13: 978-0-9856826-3-7

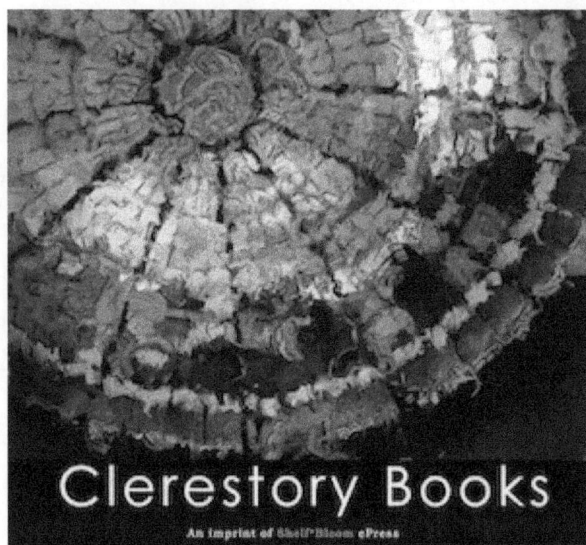

Clerestory Books

An imprint of Shelf Bloom ePress

Dedication:

With life-long appreciation to my mentors and caring companions in person and in page both in this life and the one to come.

"For we did not follow cunningly devised fables when we made known to you the power and coming of our Lord Jesus Christ, but were eyewitnesses of His majesty." 2 Peter 1:16, NKJV.

Acknowledgements

It is only through the living of this life and exposure to all of the various individuals that I have learned from over the years that a book such as this can be presented to you, the reader.

Not all of those who I have learned from will be acknowledged here. This section will simply illuminate a handful of those that have been the most pivotal and *POSITIVE* in my own life. I could not possibly recognize all who have been involved in my life long learning process without creating a multiple volume set. If you expected to be seen here and were not, please keep in mind that your inclusion in this section would not necessarily lend more credence to the impact you have made upon my life and worldview.

Learning experiences are not always positive, yet they are just as valid. In fact, I recall hearing someone once say that the *pains* of the learning experiences of life are perhaps more influential and instrumental in our choices regarding education. I would agree that the pains we experience might be the greatest catalyst for rapid learning. However, it is within our power to make those learning processes positive experiences or to respond negatively. I am grateful that I usually respond in a positive fashion and can wield useful and cohesive knowledge to assist me in living my daily life.

I have consistently and fairly reliably carried the burden of education (in all of its various forms) further than was necessary. There are many reasons for this, many of them I must acknowledge are somewhat rooted in self-gratification. Among the more noble reasons, however, include my desire to reward the teacher in the greatest way possible; by building upon the knowledge and wisdom the teacher conveys. Can any person empowered by the Holy Spirit (regardless of their spiritual maturity level) ever deny the value and joy in bringing glory to the Lord Jesus Christ in everything we say and do, including learning or teaching? Of those pursuits of learning that are somewhat self-gratifying I must recognize the self-pride inherent in the grasping of a new skill or bit of applied wisdom (whether that be the fixing of the toaster, changing the oil in a vehicle, playing catch with others or reading New Testament Greek). Also, the value of seeing another person's eyes positively light up with their recognition of a precious or beneficial point of information cannot be discounted or overlooked. Doubtlessly, there is great reward in learning and teaching.

This acknowledgement section is really intended to provide a superficial glimpse into my most direct influences and to provide a somewhat comprehensive means of thanking those who have helped to craft my worldview and, consequently, my entire life.

First and foremost, with increasing recognition and respect, I must thank the One True Creator God. Our every breath is as a result of His perfect eternal plan. And, whether a person acknowledges it or not, their every heartbeat is an increasing glory to Him. As James Hallett put it so succinctly in 1848:

"Salvation, in all its parts, branches, and hearings, is the greatest of all subjects; for it is the Alpha and the Omega of the Bible, and the Lord alone is the Author of it; as it is written, "Salvation is of God; thy blessing is upon thy people." (Ps. 3:8) And David saith, "The Lord is my light and my salvation." (Ps. 27:1) And Jonah saith, "They that pursue lying vanities forsake their own mercies, but I will pay that that I have vowed, Salvation is of the Lord." (Jonah 2:8,9)" (From *The Lord's Salvation, the Sinners Hope*).

Salvation is obviously the Alpha and Omega of the Bible and the beginning and end of meaningful human life.

In specific, I cannot help but recognize the role the Apostle Paul played in the furtherance of the truths of Christ in the daily lives of mankind, even in these 2 millennia since the writings of his dear epistles. The various literary contributions of C.R Stam, C.F. Baker, Pastor Paul Sadler, Dr. E. Campbell, Ron Merryman, A.T. Robertson, Robert B. Thieme, Jr., Rollin Wilson, W. Edward Bedore, and J.C. O'Hair all played a great part in the formal foundation of my spiritual understanding.

As time has progressed, men such as Francis Schaeffer, Dr. Robert A. Cook and C.S. Lewis have also (in various degrees and means) contributed to my Spiritual viewpoint, compassion and daily walk in this world (while not becoming a part of the world). As C.S. Lewis pointed out:

"I believe in Christianity as I believe that the sun has risen: not only because I see it, but because by it I see everything else."

3

As one builds a spiritual foundation, particularly one based upon objective truth, they must use that foundation as a frame of reference or become hypocritical (or spiritually stagnant). As that frame of reference is utilized, an increasing number of life events suddenly become learning experiences until you can no longer consider any worthwhile life event not being a spiritual learning experience, praise God!

Gary DeMar, Dr. Robert Nix and Christian Overman all formally contributed in the provision of the basic constructs of an expanding view of self-government and the role of God in that expansion.

The various writings of J. Gresham Machen & Richard N. Davies continuously prove the value of education regardless of the age of said truth or of the original presentation (true wisdom and knowledge is timeless). Their writings directly encouraged me to continue on in this quest to complete this humble work of mine.

Dr. Mel Mulder and Dr. Henry Morris (among others) who inspire great confidence and value in the Word and the full respect of its literal rendering of history.

David Breese and Dave Hunt provided the initial guidance necessary to begin to have all of these sources of information to come together in a cohesive way, pointing towards the root of the problems seen in every city block and every country byway throughout all of God's creation.

Bryce D. Confair has singlehandedly been the greatest influence upon all of these realms. As we have learned together through these years, building-up together as brothers in the Body (he doing the lion's share of the effort), he encouraged a spiritually rudderless young man to become an individual who increases in wisdom, understanding, respect of God, and appreciation of those things eternal and currently unseen. He has been the emotion and spirit of my learning and I will always thank him. What a joy to spend eternity together glorifying God and working in His service! Before even Bryce, however, his dear wife Patricia Ann gave me the spark & initial consideration to find enjoyment in learning about the Creator of the entire universe and His truth, morality and value.

All of these (as well as so many others that cannot be named here for sake of space & the reader's attention) have been my mentors in person and page. And, as is part of the beauty of learning and influence, their individual educations, backgrounds and influences all impact me (in their various degrees) as well.

What man could honestly do any good for anyone if it was not for his patient, caring, loving and willing life companions? Therefore, I am also honored to thank those who have stuck with me through thick and thin and along all the rapids and riffles of learning about life. I want to thank first those two people who chose to give a family a chance -- my father and mother. My parents placed within me the importance of self-learning. Both of them had roles to play that have proven beneficial over the years; my father who seemingly demanded so very much and my mother who gently encouraged me so very well. Their different types of love blended together to help create that which I am today and will be for years to come. My wife, Sandra, who is the love of my life and a dear sister in the Body, she is the one I rely upon most of all. Perhaps the best way to illustrate her impact on my life is this: she has encouraged me to carry on in spite of my various challenges, she has made me laugh and has constantly reminded me of joy. She has done so much to ease the negativity in life and has given me an outlet for my purpose. She increasingly demonstrates the helper every man yearns for.

A special thank you to my sisters and grandparents who all directly helped to teach me the value of cooperation, honor, duty, and chivalry (even if it didn't seem like it at the time!).

And – finally -- to my particular friend, Jason Monroe, my contemporary who has truly never turned his back on me nor our dear Savior Jesus Christ, even though I have greatly challenged him (sometimes beyond that which he thought he could bear). Jason, I so very look forward to our continued ministry to each other both in this life and the next.

Preface

Your humble author has compiled, written and edited this volume during the years 2013 and 2014. These years are in marked contrast to the original authorship and publication of the book *Seven Men Who Rule the World from the Grave* by David W. Breese, which was published in 1990 by Moody Press in Chicago (Hardcover ISBN 0-8024-8449-2; Paperback ISBN 0-8024-8448-4).

There was an obvious need for the creation of a follow-up and contemporary approach to the original work of Pastor Breese, a compulsion made all the more acute by the increasingly inane actions of an increasingly spiritually insensible humanity as illuminated by the even more inane mass media & entertainment establishment.

There is no doubt that when Pastor Breese originally penned his work in the Reagan/Bush presidential years, his scholarship and logical thought process was solid and worthwhile. However, as with all things, time alters the landscape that men like Dave Breese had access to view. It will, no doubt, be the same for this volume as well if but given time.

In light of the fact of a continually changing social and historical landscape, I have provided this companion and independent addendum to his invaluable book. The short book that you are now reading will make infinitely more sense and will appear more complete should you have read (or should you find yourself reading for any reason) the original book by Dave Breese (hereby referred to in this book as *Seven Men*).

The facts and men presented by Mr. Breese are accurate and largely beyond reproach. This volume you are now reading does little to criticize or improve upon his original effort in *Seven Men*. Instead, it is intended to cement those tenants in light of events generated since the original publishing of his book and illuminate further vital information since transpired. Since the original publishing of the book, there has been a very specific set of events that have allowed the further growth and metastasizing of the research and development of Satan, which is defined via various means by our increasingly depraved society. **The purpose of the research and development of Satan is to usurp the universe from the long-suffering Sovereign**

Creator God. Mankind (as a corporate whole) is, either via willing complicity or foolishness, promoting or perpetuating the plan developed by the head of all evil: Satan. This is the master conspiracy of all conspiracies and the root cause of the myriad of atrocities and distractions in our modern age.

Whenever any person; regardless of pursuit, education, experience, age, gender, ethnicity, race or political alliance believes they can accomplish something outside of the bounds, enablement and empowerment of the Sovereign Creator God and his guiding Word, they are following the action plan of Satan himself.

To that end I encourage you to read this short volume, to study it for yourself, to reconsider the daily events that once seemed so normal and disconnected from each other and to recognize the personal necessity that is the person and resurrected Messiah for all of mankind; Jesus Christ.

CHAPTER 1

The original intent of *Seven Men* was to educate readers regarding a series of past events and historical figures that were involved (either knowingly or unknowingly) in the attack upon and eventual destruction of various individual components of our society that, once united and intertwined as a united front of battle, would equate to the complete and total destruction of a once God-fearing society of Christian individuals. Mr. Breese obviously intended to ingrain in the reader the importance of adhering to a Biblical worldview on an individual basis so that society, as a whole, would flourish. This viewpoint is held in direct opposition to a humanistic (human amplifying) worldview that denies God and will be responsible for the destruction of society.

Some people would correctly call this a *conspiracy*. And amongst those who would consider labeling these events and the men driving them as a conspiracy, a great number of readers of *Seven Men* would say so only in a derogatory - tongue-in-cheek – way. That is, they would assume the facetious approach to the subject, quickly eliminating the possibility that such a conspiracy actually does, and obviously must, exist. For those readers, I hope this companion causes them to pause, reread the original volume and reconsider their facetious approach.

Other readers take the subject of the volume seriously, considering a conspiracy as it actually is, as defined by Webster's 1913:

A combination of men for an evil purpose; an agreement, between two or more persons, to commit a crime in concert, as treason; a plot.

Only, this master conspiracy is the foundational basis for all other conspiracies both real and imagined. It is a conspiracy mastered and coordinated by a supernatural entity who has but one purpose and goal, to conquer the universe and destroy the glory, beauty and value of the original creation while usurping the power of the original

Creator, assuming all meaningful power for himself. That is the singular paramount goal of Satan.

And, for those readers who already recognize this fact, this companion will reinforce and validate their Biblical Worldview approach to both history and current events while pointing out other thoughts and components that Mr. Breese did not originally include but that, by historical deduction and Biblical thought, have risen as the unifying pieces of the individual attack fronts in the battle against the truth of the Word of God and His Sovereign reign. The foundational technology needed to bring increasing prosperity to the cause of Satan (albeit temporarily) has been introduced, is being actively developed and even appears to be a source of obsession and worship.

Perhaps *Seven Men* would have been better entitled "Seven Reasonably Modern Men Who Rule the World from the Grave". At no point does Breese attempt to perpetuate the thought that, historically, there are *ONLY* seven men who have driven society to its current status and the increasingly destructive future that it is actively accelerating towards. There are, by necessity, far more than simply seven men in the pursuit of the wishful success of the conspiracy of Satan over the course of the history of mankind. However, the roots of the variously destructive modern intellectual, philosophical, religious, and political means of perverted persuasion were well expressed and developed in the seven men Breese points out in his book.

Before I continue, it is of great importance that the reader realizes that the only way to prohibit yourself from being a willing accomplice in this conspiracy of Satan's design is to ally yourself solely with the Lord Jesus Christ. If you have not made this choice as of yet, you may find yourself unwilling or unable to fully recognize the breadth and depth of the conspiracy and its evil end. In a nutshell, you will need to have begun developing a Biblical worldview in order to truly come to a better understanding of how and why this is occurring as it is.

It really does come down to worldview. And, your worldview will be either Biblical, humbling yourself before the Sovereign Creator God of the Bible alone, or you will develop a secular worldview. A secular worldview is any worldview that does not view the events of the world and its history through the boundaries and clarity set forth in the Word (the Holy Bible) as inspired by God alone.

Simply put, *Seven Men* addresses the basic viewpoint, frame of reference or "worldview" of a person that impacts the daily management and operating decisions of their own lives, and subsequently, the lives of others around them. This worldview philosophy is a vital component of the functionality of the self-government of each individual.

As each person practices their worldview philosophy whether knowingly (active) or unknowingly (passively) upon their own lives; they, through basic self-confidence established through mitigated risk and experience, then begin using the relative "wisdom" created by the practice of their worldview (whether they employ genuinely actual wisdom or just a type of self-deluding "wisdom"). This applied knowledge is then directly employed in an increasing amount of interpersonal experiences. If these interpersonal experiences are self-gratifying, then the person continues to emotionally reinforce and empirically fortify their worldview. This system can either be used to increase their harmony with the Scriptures and the Holy Spirit, therefore directly increasing their fellowship with the Lord ("running the race, keeping the faith") or they will reinforce their humanistic and hedonistic tendencies and increasingly alienate themselves from the truth of the Word and the daily interaction of the Holy Spirit ("they, having their conscience seared as with a hot iron").

It is commonly seen that those people who are adrift on the sea of life (so-to-speak) are swayed by the winds of aggressive philosophies. In those cases, the further or longer adrift, the more accepting the wayward sailor is of having their course directed by any wind, regardless of direction. Of course, any traveler through life would prefer to have their course directed by a temperate breeze that ever hastens their arrival to the port they would best describe as "paradise", especially if they see the alternative of themselves being driven onto the rocks of a lee shore by a gusty and violent windstorm.

It is through and by this basic system of human reasoning (many describe it as "the path of least resistance") that most people operate. And, as a direct result, the substantive portion of the population of humanity is easily swayed into action (or, potentially, inaction) by the most temperate, steady, and self-gratifying winds of philosophy and worldview.

It is precisely because of these facts that the subject of worldview is one of the foundation stones of living the Christian life. It is the intrinsic and fundamental values provided by a Biblical worldview, directed as closely by the Word, the Holy Spirit and fellowship in the Body of Christ as is possible in this day and age, that we must first recognize, then embrace, and then employ to communicate and minister to others, regardless of their current worldview. Breese does an exceptional job of illustrating these tenants.

Seven Men, distills the modern worldview philosophy and methodology to two camps: a secular worldview and a Biblical worldview. It is from this approach that we begin to learn about those men who practiced their non-Biblical viewpoint while yet living to create a storm of humanistic delusion that would ensure the blowing of the winds of change for generations to come. These winds of change direct men into waters containing dangerous shoals and encourage the foundering of both the physical lives of men as well as their eternal Spiritual lives.

Therefore, it is quite appropriate that the book, following the preface and introduction, focuses upon the origin of the greatest secular challenge to the basic truth of the creation of the universe. If society (as encouraged by Satan) can undermine the basic truth of the creation by the one and true Sovereign Creator of the universe, then they can call the entire Bible invalid or less than fully valid when compared to (or in light of) humanistic philosophy and scientific empirical research/study/theory.

The first chapter of *Seven Men* clearly demonstrates that Charles Darwin intended to cause the destruction of God through his "theory" and "science". Darwin doubted the veracity of the simple Bible message largely due to his practiced and increasingly established secular worldview and negative volitional response to the true gospel of Jesus Christ. In this way, Charles Darwin, by attempting to answer questions while ignoring basic logical truths evident in the Word, chased after his self-gratifying pursuit of knowledge and began blowing the winds most destructive (and distracting!) to the modern concept of our true Sovereign God (and, in truth, appearing to "invalidate" His Word) and scientific research today.

The ramifications of this pursuit as initially propelled by one man have now become an obsession by billions of people. This obsession distracts people from having peace and contentedness in the basic truths of the Word and via their reconciled fellowship in the Holy Spirit. It also steals our appreciation and awesome wonderment of the creation from the only truth of the One who created it. This, in turn, drives society to spend unimaginable funds on hollow pursuits to explain that which can be simply explained and properly understood in a Holy book that can, today, be purchased in a dollar store. They do this in the pursuit of peace, contentedness and knowledge; assuming that once the proper level of secular theory and science is achieved the winds first blown by Darwin will lead their ship into the port called Utopia.

And, it is these fits, frustrations and motivations that confound those with a secular worldview. For, it is impossible for them to ever reach the port that they seek while they strain of their own effort to reach that port. The winds that Darwin first rustled and millions have encouraged blow one within the range of hope to reach their perfect destination, but will always lead them to one side or another and either side equates to destruction.

So much thought is wasted, so much financial capital is thrown aside for no redeeming eternal purpose, and so much life is made forfeit. Darwin did not find proper satisfaction in his own life nor will anyone else that has any truly objective and logical consideration by the day of their death and has rejected the truth of the Word and have at least begun to embrace the Biblical worldview that corresponds to that simple, perfect and complete truth.

The preface and introduction of *Seven Men* should not be skipped or quickly glanced over as it provided some glimpses of what the reader can expect to encounter and what Breese will undoubtedly expound upon in the rest of the volume.

The following portion, found on page 10, is an excellent example of the necessary attitude when studying *Seven Men*. It is a commandment that many have often considered, but perhaps not in the light in which it had been provided in this volume:

"In fact, there is a sense in which the command "Thou shalt have no other gods before me" is not finally a command but rather a devastating, simple statement of diamond-hard reality. It is a total absolute, nonnegotiable in the slightest aspect. It is not altered by rhetoric, softened by tears, weakened by reflection, eroded by time, cowed by resentment, or defeated by successive waves of frantic assault by legions of froth-mouthed enemies."

Page 18 provided this outstanding and profound statement, which provides great obvious value through its veracity:

"Conversely, to have a correct view of man, God, and history is the key to sanity and survival for individual men and for the entire culture."

Page 24 illustrates an interesting passage from the pen of Mr. William Sullivan, the author of the introduction of the 1972 reprinting of the Darwin diary, Sullivan here is referring to the diary:

"This book was prelude to what became probably the most revolutionary change that has ever occurred in man's view of himself."

And it is this little bit of text that caused me the greatest amusement and alarm, simultaneously. For, it is an obviously heinous statement, when considered in the light of any one of the many saints in the Body of Christ. There are many who have introspectively considered themselves prior to their reconciliation to God when compared to their reconciled and sanctified eternal existence following their reconciliation through conversion and spiritual transformation. And, in truth, that is – by leaps and bounds - the most revolutionary change that has ever occurred in man's view of himself (a revolutionary change that God Himself committed unto man through Jesus Christ alone).

Some other bits will undoubtedly be found useful, as they encapsulate various individual thoughts that cross the minds of many individuals. For example, the secular repudiation of the Pre-Darwinist past and that Darwin, in a sense, restarted history.

CHAPTER 2

The second chapter of *Seven Men*, is entitled "Thinking Further About Science".

It is quite obvious that it is of great importance that a secular humanity be made capable of distinguishing the truth beyond the hype of what is widely purported to be science (and which is – largely – the overzealous pursuit of humanism). And, it is of the most vital importance that Bible believing Christians see through the thinly veiled lies, half-truths and foolishness of evolutionary science.

This chapter of *Seven Men* begins to chip away at the façade of science, which purports to be the end all-be all response providing supposedly undeniable truth to all of mankind. However, it does not take a deep file or chisel, nor many blows of a hammer to first examine the apparent cracks and then break away the layers of self-delusion, illogical tendency and faulty empirical wisdom found in most modern "science". This exposes the weaknesses and obvious faith based (not faith in the true Creator God, but in their own human powers) thought processes of what our western worldview exalts above all other sources of philosophy – that is – science.

As *Seven Men* begins to provide a systematic approach to presenting data regarding the house of cards which our secular society is built upon, we find a slight pause in chapter two to frame and recognize the importance of the "discipline" of science in the well-established modern day western worldview philosophy. For, one specific truth regarding the science-worship of the modern era that cannot be ignored regards the origin of the worship of science and the long-reaching ramifications of such a pursuit. This chapter provides us with a basic introduction to the subject. Those introductory points will expand as we continue forward through the text.

Ultimately, it is impossible for a Bible believing and RESPECTING individual to place science at the same level of truth as the Word. And God forbid a believer placing a superior position of truth and faith in science as though science has authority over the Word. If science and the Bible are in conflict with one another, regardless of the topic of conversation or the apparent rational/empirical information presented regarding the matter, the

Word of God must always rise above anything human created or presented as truth outside of the Word of God. For, as we read:

"Because the foolishness of God is wiser than men, and the weakness of God is stronger than men." 1 Corinthians 1:25, NKJV.

And, it is obvious that the Word is perfect and complete, capable of all instruction into righteousness. This is our calling in this day and age:

"All Scripture is given by inspiration of God, and is profitable for doctrine, for reproof, for correction, for instruction in righteousness, that the man of God may be complete, thoroughly equipped for every good work." 2 Timothy 3:16, 17, NKJV.

It is beginning here that Breese is obviously disadvantaged compared to the world today, as 25 years of history has been added to the textbooks since his publishing.

It is because of this fact that I can suggest a few superficial disagreements with the text that must be addressed and kept in mind by the modern reader of this book:

1) Figure 4 on page 38. This figure attempts to portray the "Christian Cultural Impact" failing/ceasing at a point in the future (clearly the direct result of the printing of this volume being done in 1990, as 25 years has now passed since the text was revised. The author might have very well agreed with my current assessment but he cannot be asked today as he passed away into glory in 2002). I would contend that the "cultural" impact of Christianity has failed/ceased (as Francis Schaeffer did coin it a "post-Christian" society). We are now - at best - individually impacting in this current society and age. I cannot recognize any meaningful cultural impact that true Bible believing Christianity is gaining (or truly not rapidly retreating from, for that matter) upon our current base of population. This is, obviously, impossible to prove and will be so until the end of history, at which time we can determine the actual end date of widespread and authentic Christian cultural impact. But, at that time, the debate would be purely academic anyhow, with no real necessity for the information.

2) Consider the following phrase: "That respect has now, however, led society into a dangerous attitude, an attitude that comes close to making a god out of science." It appears obvious that science

is already a (the?) god amongst the hoi polloi/mass populace (and this issue is likely directly due to the relative age of the volume). Most of the secular society we reside aside of in this age already believe anything and everything that science provides to mankind, regardless of its validity/veracity. As proof of this obsession-worship, we see those scientific findings vacillating between extremes, and the populace following right along with those oscillations, rarely asking why the wavering occurs or exists in the first place. They simply choose to "go with the flow".

Something else that has been proven time and time again through history is mankind's endless pursuit of equality with God. From the moment the serpent first appeared in the garden to Eve, we see him trying to tempt Eve with God-like equality. Satan offered the twisted and false opportunity and Eve bit. Now, all of natural mankind is afflicted with the terminal illness called "imparted/imputed sin". This is a basic truth all men are convicted of in their heart of hearts and is something they would rather figuratively choose to plug their ears and yell "LA-LA-LA-LA-LA" than to choose to listen to the still small voice and follow the true Creator God of the universe. Science willingly distracts mankind and they increasingly crave that distraction and the self-deluding philosophy it establishes in the heart of those foolish enough to adhere to that destructive satanic philosophy.

Science (as practiced by those without a respect for the Sovereign Creator God) is the latest manifestation of the pursuit of Godliness. Furthermore, it is the direct replacement for the truth of the Word, in direct competition for the hearts and minds of men. And, since so many Christians refuse to take on their responsibility to the truth of the Word and the cause of Christ; science is appears to be the god mankind needed/wanted and is in large part the driving factor behind the hedonism and Godlessness we are currently experiencing in this global society.

Public education is intentionally attempting (and currently succeeding) at destroying any message other than the information provided by flawed human empirical wisdom. And, the author states something on page 45, which illuminates the absolute folly of that endeavor:

"Wisdom begins when we come to know Christ, in whom are hidden all of the treasures of wisdom and knowledge."

Mankind is choosing to refuse to worship God when they choose, instead, to worship mankind and their "scientific" philosophy and western worldview (you cannot serve two masters, see: Matthew 6:24). Mankind believes - as a collective consciousness - that their morality and justice can supersede that of Godly wisdom (which they invalidate the sheer existence of) and His perfect plan (and I do not mean to indicate a "figurative" meaning here, I do mean that they believe this quite literally in every sense). They assume that they will eventually usurp God (or at least totally wield the power that historical society had equated with "God") and, once that act is completed, they will then also steal His glory for themselves, leaving God shattered and destroyed on the highway of history and the desolate plains of saccharine philosophy.

Science is but one stone in the foundation of humanism; humanism is designed and wielded to destroy spiritual truth in this day and age while amplifying man above God.

In closing for this chapter, I provide this quote:

A man can no more diminish God's glory by refusing to worship Him than a lunatic can put out the sun by scribbling the word, 'darkness' on the walls of his cell. – C.S. Lewis

CHAPTER 3

Chapter 3 of *Seven Men* is a short chapter, even when compared to the length of the other chapters already summarized previous. It deals with the methodology of Darwin's role in influencing from the grave.

Entitled *Social Darwinism*, the chapter title, by itself, is a harbinger of the text to follow. This title – comprised of only two words – is really sufficient to make a series of logical mental leaps based upon the text previously experienced. And, coupled with what I must say is an obvious societal movement in the exact direction Mr. Breese anticipated a quarter century ago, it is beyond speculation that this component of his theory/philosophy has overwhelming rational and empirical basis.

Social Darwinism is unfolding right before our very eyes. It has actively made a foothold in essentially all realms of social thinking. The masses have adopted it as part of their thought process and they now cannot imagine considering any volitional decision making processes without incorporating this system of reasoning. They do this quite naturally and without question. Satan has laid the trap and mankind, by and large, has fallen lock step into his diabolical manipulation of intrinsic thought and social engineering.

Social Darwinism is being introduced to children from the first tender moments of their life, usually without question and in myriad of ways. Those little newborn children may not recognize or realize the implications of this worldly viewpoint (most life-experienced adults do not recognize or realize them either), but a lack of recognition or realization does not trump the existence of such thought processes or eliminate the damage done by them.

There is a yearning for knowledge within every human being causing them to ask questions such as,

"Where did I come from?", "Why am I here?", or, "How did humanity get to this moment?".

Even children at a very young age experience these questions that seem to spring forth from their innermost person. In this current society that we live in, many of these children are exposed daily to members of our society whose responses to those questions destroy the possibility of the existence of the true Sovereign Creator God. In this way, not only do these people lead children into destruction by their propaganda (usually widely termed as "enlightenment", "knowledge", or by various versions of "philosophy" and "science"), the actions of those with a God destructive worldview prove their desire and strategic necessity to deny the true Creator God. They do this through the methods of social Darwinism.

Disrespect of God is everywhere. It can easily be found in homes, in schools (including running rampant in post-secondary education), in Girl Scout and Boy Scout meetings, and yes, even in "churches" or on so-called "Christian" radio and television stations. Rarely does a school board meeting or city council meeting not display either the open and outright continued indoctrination of social Darwinism or something even more insidious. Perhaps most dangerous and telling: these agents of change and evil indoctrination simply operate from a standpoint of having already been nearly perfected by their own indoctrination. As the old adage goes, "actions speak louder than words", and the self-propagating error of humanism based upon a demonic foundation continues not only upon lofty words but also by incalculable action. That demonic foundation rests partially (but wholly necessarily) upon social Darwinism.

Social Darwinism requires that we explain away God. However, its desire is even more treacherous than that. It drives, desires, demands cultures to eliminate the entire thought of God from our hearts and minds. The only way that they believe they will ever be successful in this endeavor is to begin the process of eliminating God from any conscious thought of even the youngest of the children in our society. Our world governments have actively been implementing a plan of attack for generations, but that plan has only recently begun to take identifiable shape.

Only within the last generation has the desire of implementing the philosophy of social Darwinism met the logistical components necessary to actually implement that desire on a massive and efficient scale. A godless government needs to demonstrate that "ideal" and "utopian" social structures are engineered and controlled by impersonal forces. They cannot leave God in control of any realm or it will be the undoing of their hope of ushering in their own type of hedonistic humanist utopia opportunity. Satan has offered them their poisoned apple and humanity is once again buying into the most ancient lie; the lie that says: "But thou shalt not not surely die."

Let me clarify that mankind does not, in the majority at least at this point in history, even recognize that their entire thought process and frame of reference has been hijacked by Satan and his demonic plan. This does not erase the responsibility of mankind in the discussion, however (for God provided mankind with the opportunity and responsibility of freewill). Any person who, by the mere virtue of any personally practiced mental or emotional establishment of any philosophy, knowledge or morality not completely respecting the Word of God or even basic humility before God, chooses to embrace any information contrary to God and what He has communicated to us through the Holy Bible. Therefore, they - actively or passively - reject the wisdom of God (who is omniscient and Sovereign) and favor the wisdom of man. This is a textbook example of how Satan works best in social circles.

It is obvious that we are not living in an improving age of social enlightenment (regardless of what humanists may try to present). Every possible sign points to the failures of a massaging and manipulative human spirit with satanic support with a goal of control, indoctrination and distraction from the Gospel of Jesus Christ. Yet, the social environment mankind has helped Satan to create prohibits them from not only recognizing the failure of their actions (at least on a scale affecting large portions of humanity) but also eliminates the questioning about the motivations and level of success from even being uttered (and perhaps even personally considered). Ultimately, the proponents of social Darwinism desire (and, in truth, demand) that there be no question of this philosophy. They want people, from the most tender and innocent of age, to not even question the established façade of reality that they have ushered in. Only then can they, with no limits, control all of humanity to do their bidding. Only then will mankind be truly under the command of all of the evil forces allied against God Himself.

The disciples of this social Darwinist agenda are not fearful of what God may do to them as a result of their intentional sins against Him. They truly believe God is irrelevant because He does not exist, or, perhaps even more horrifyingly, they assume that they can become greater than He is. Look at this quote:

"The Bible is not merely another book ... it has and remains an incredibly dangerous book. ... I am convinced that the battle for humankind's future must be waged and won in the public classroom by teachers who correctly perceive their role as the proselytizers of a new faith. ... These teachers must embody the same dedication as the most rabid fundamentalist preachers, for they will be ministers of another sort, utilizing a classroom instead of a pulpit to convey humanist values in whatever subject they teach. ... The classroom must and will become an arena of conflict between the old and the new – the rotting corpse of Christianity, together with all its adjacent evils and misery, and the new faith of humanism, resplendent in its promise of a world in which the never-realized Christian ideal of love thy neighbor will finally be achieved." -- John Dunphy, "A Religion for a New Age"

I challenge you to present this quote to any university professor and ask them if they largely agree or disagree with the thought process of Mr. Dunphy. Then, consider how many young and powerful minds they encounter annually while they are paid substantial sums to continue the indoctrination of those valuable members of society into a philosophy denying our Creator and His wonderful gift of life (both temporal and eternal) to the very humanity that denies Him.

There is no debate that social Darwinism is thriving, that mankind continues to ignore the truth to grasp a more enticing lie, and that parents increasingly not only do not mind this fact, they encourage this type of destructive indoctrination.

Social Darwinism is amongst us. It has not only forced the gates, it has set up shop and has taken its hold upon our homes and places of faith. Worse than this, it has begun to fill the hearts and minds of the mass of human society.

The only means to combat this disease is to inoculate the people with the only actual perfect truth found in the existence of the universe: God and His plan, His Purpose, His Word through the Lord Jesus Christ.

If this inoculation is not accomplished, there can be no hope to cease this satanic invasion of the human mind and soul individually that then coordinates so effectively in a broad social sense.

CHAPTER 4

This chapter in *Seven Men* begins to provide a glimpse into the long-reaching ramifications of a socialist/communist society as penned, in large part, by Karl Marx.

I must admit that, as the chapter began and for the first several pages, I had a rising concern considering the content of the chapter. Not due solely to the content itself, but largely due to my inability to really recognize any proper or applicable avenues to convey my thoughts and assimilation of the chapter. Just as I was beginning to really wonder how I would convert my reading into learning, Mr. Breese raised a proverbial intellectual 4 x 4 pressure treated post and slammed it directly into my blockheaded brain. The ultimate personal culmination of this chapter truly occurred on pages 68 and 69.

Truth be told, although I am well aware of the necessity of learning about the role Marx has played in this current societal situation we find ourselves in, I do find it discouraging that we have so much information about his life and thought processes (as evidenced by the word by word presentation of part of his eulogy). And, that so much time in "civilized" society is given to his philosophies (truly a form of insanity as demonstrated and explained by Mr. Breese). As I consider an estimate of the number of hours of collective human energy (mental/educational/financial) provided daily to the existence and error filled insanity of Karl Marx and compare it to that energy expelled by mankind in the study of our glorious risen Savior Jesus Christ in our current society, I do feel a sense of sorrow.

While we study the culmination of the "philosophy" of Marxism, we must study the *man* (or, the outward appearance of) who was Karl Marx. However, it is obvious that the thoughts he penned were not solely his own and that others had proceeded him in various thought components and influenced his life and writings. Some of those were openly acknowledged while others may not be clearly displayed through the magnifying glass of history. Marx was just a man, a man with a type of insanity, as any person rejecting the Creator God suffers from. As a man Marx was emotionally controlled, manipulated and convinced. Was this manipulation solely via the human sprit and intellect alone, or is there a greater supernatural power at work here?

Is there a coordinated strategy with an ultimate purpose? Of course there is and that purpose is undeniably diabolical.

As stated in the chapter previous, this diabolical purpose does not eliminate the culpability of mankind and, in the specific example in this chapter: Karl Marx. Instead, it makes Marx/mankind all the more culpable. For they knew the truth in their heart, as they did from their infancy (God has placed a conscience within each man as well as the freewill to ignore and corrupt that conscience). They chose to deny and usurp God.

It is obvious that mankind has exchanged the truth for a lie (Romans 1). And, when the case for truth is laid out so clearly to humanity via the inspired writers of the Word of God and they can use aids to learning such as the example we are discussing here (*Seven Men*), I seriously wonder how any logical thinker not completely confused or consumed by the diabolical plan of Satan could embrace a concept such as Marxism. But, it is important to recall the discussion provided by Breese on page 68 regarding sanity vs. insanity and increasing depravity (which is reinforced by the short-term gratification of the human morality by Satan). To know that we are (at the very least) on the event horizon of such a demoralizing time in human history (especially when compared to the recent culturally Christian past of our nation -again see Francis Schaeffer – namely, *Death in the City*) is sobering. However, we are commanded to rejoice in all things, and that will we do as patriotic citizens of the Heavenly places (Philippians 3). Our glory is so exceeding and transcendent in not only the current time but in eternity as well. We will judge angels (I Corinthians 6), we will be in the very presence of He who alone can absolutely define truth, hope and love. Not as we would describe them, but as they truly are in perfection. What a blessing, what a hope! In this present time we are to represent this to all of an increasingly depraved humanity.

It seems as though there is no end to the acceleration of depravity in our global society today. There is no doubt that Marxism, in all of its forms, greatly fuels this acceleration. Marxism requires enrichment by atheism to function as designed. In fact, it is impossible for socialism to exist in practice without the total invalidation of the soul found within each member of humanity. The only "religion" left in place via Marxism is an empty shell used simply as a means of latent control.

Karl Marx, and his "intellectual" proponents all assume that the world is devoid of God. Their assumption is necessary to ensure that the morality of God and His mighty plan becomes discredited within the craving spirit of mankind. If the image of God is defeated, then any information regarding God is discredited, and mankind must turn to itself as a means of coping with the rigors of life. Once the masses turn to humanism as a means of hurdling the gulf of spirituality found within each person from the most tender of ages, then will a certain small segment of society be in full control of all of the population.

However, the motivations of Marx and his followers referred to in this passage remain, ultimately, unanswered:

"To Marx the individual counted for nothing and was only significant as he functioned for the good of society... the greatest good was that which advanced the Marxist society." (page 70)

Ultimately, as I considered the chapter, I still find myself wondering what the gratification or true root of motivation is behind this system of thought and societal control? I find it hard to assume that a Marxist/Socialist would work their entire life to usher in their perfect, utopian world government system only to have their own life perish and that they will cease to exist or recognize an ever transcendent society devoid of God and amplifying mankind. What is the point in their innermost mental recesses? In simpler terms, what is in it for them? Is it the temporal feeling of being a component of a utopian god-like existence? Do they delude themselves to the point of feeling self-righteous while living? If so, they are completely confused and distracted from the reality.

The collective society of Marxism is nothing more than a gathering of individuals. However, the individual counts for nothing in a Marxist society. If the individual counts for nothing, then why do anything for a collective society? What is the purpose? What is the motivation? There can be no society without first having the individuals to make up the society. It is a conundrum that is not answered by this chapter and may not actually be answerable by any person on this earth.

As an outsider looking in at the socialist movement, I find it easy to see that Satan drives humanity in this regard. He is not only capable but also willing to drive man over the spiritual cliff in his desire to attain a power greater than God. Mankind is being used in this endeavor and socialism (and, capitalism to a lesser degree) is an actual manifestation of this strategy.

But what is the ultimate hope of a Marxist? What will cause them redeeming self-gratification?

An error that many people in our modern American society make is to assume that we are locked into a battle of socialism vs. capitalism. Of course, this is a straw-man argument. The truth is that God is neither socialist nor capitalist. Both socialism and capitalism is materialism in some form, neither of which is something that God could possibly strive for since he already has dominion over the entire universe. This debate is not based solely in an economic realm; it is most largely based and operating in a spiritual realm with physical manifestations.

Discredit God, invalidate true Spirituality, eliminate those amongst the masses who disagree with the humanist agenda, amplify mankind, place Satan fully in control at the head of humanity (eventually in a physical, tangible body), and overthrow God. That is the skeleton of the program in place via this train of thought. Of course, the shocking moment for humanity as a whole will come when the overthrow of God never occurs and instead mankind will be left holding the proverbial bag. Satan will never wrest control from the Sovereign Creator God and never could (God is sovereign, omniscient, omnipotent). Satan is, without challenger, the most deluded existence in the universe. However, he is not averse to continuing to attempt to outlast, outwit and outplay God for control of all creation. Until his utter destruction he will desire the depravity of humanity if but for a temporal period.

As we read on page 69, "What remains is the philosophic cadaver of a body without a soul." That is the true and perversely cultivated legacy of Karl Marx. That legacy will eventually take only one possible manifestation. Contrary to what many today believe, that manifestation will not be a utopian socialist society. It will be, it must be, total depravity fully embracing the plan of Satan.

CHAPTER 5

Chapter 5 of *Seven Men* cements the long-reaching ramifications of a socialist/communist society as penned, in large part, by Karl Marx and initially presented/discussed in chapter four.

To begin this chapter I will start at the ending of chapter five of Breese's work being discussed. For, it was at the ending that I was reminded of something that I often attempt to explain to and yet find myself forgetting to keep in mind from time to time. The particular snippet of the book I found to be the catalyst to this thought process was this:

"Beware! It may be more than a poltergeist." (Page 86)

To begin illustrating my point, I next offer a quote from C.S. Lewis (with my emphasis upon the first half of the provided quote):

"There are no ordinary people. **You have never talked to a mere mortal.** Nations, cultures, arts, civilizations – these are mortal, and their life is to ours as the life of a gnat. But it is immortals whom we joke with, work with, marry, snub and exploit – immortal horrors or everlasting splendors. This does not mean that we are to be perpetually solemn. We must play. But our merriment must be of that kind (and it is, in fact, the merriest kind) which exists between people who have, from the outset, taken each other seriously—no flippancy, no superiority, no presumption." C.S. Lewis

Now, I cannot personally ask Clive Staples Lewis if he meant to also imply that there is the possibility that an active supernatural presence (either demonic or Holy) might be intertwined with the immortal soul of every man, influencing his/her actions. However, as we can see in the depiction of the man of the tombs (Mark 5), it not only possible but has been historically accepted and demonstrated that demonic forces can invade the physical body of a person and change their entire personality, mentality and character as well as their physical attributes. Another example would be such as the demon filled man in Acts 19. We also look to the future in which the time of the tribulation, etc. depicts such possession.

The full depravity of man has the likely potential to be completely intrinsic & inherently great. But, a depraved naturally born body and mind is even more greatly evil and destructive when a supernatural spirit of evil is upon that body/mind/human spirit. Without having particular knowledge that can promise accuracy in this regard (therefore making this largely speculative), I find it to be an easy assumption that particularly evil individuals as depicted in the relatively recent history of humanity may have also been indwelt with a demonic influence that heaps a type of supernatural evil/immorality upon those who are increasingly depraved, causing a form of even greater depravity and a whole new level of wickedness, cruelty and abomination.

Our Apostle Paul warns of seducing doctrines of devils. It is obvious that these demonic forces can influence and have the motivation to do so. Something that is even more horrifying is that these demons, though not immortal, have yet to experience their destruction. Their "ministry" - which has a mission that would be the definition of advancing pure evil – spans the generations of mankind, from before the creation of man (for they fell with Satan) throughout all generations and even today. These demons exist naturally unseen in their current form. They perform surveillance on mankind. They have the power to influence and manipulate a willing human body/mind/soul. In this way, they are constantly experimenting, observing & improving their means and methods to promote the overall strategy of Satan who is their chief and superior officer.

Each person has a life that is relatively short in the overall arc of history. We cannot hope to have, when considered solely naturally, the means to (without the empowerment of a reconciled relationship with God through Christ and with an indwelling, sealing Holy Spirit) compete with the power and influence of demons due to many reasons, not the least of which is our limited lifespan. One day all demons will be defeated and cast into the lake of fire along with Satan. In the meantime, their power, influence and capability is refined and enriched with their practice, failures and successes amongst humanity.

I propose that some of those humans who may have been directly influenced by demons to propel a specific philosophy/Satanic program can be seen throughout history. In specific, I must consider the actions of Hitler (as just one simple example) and if he could have, without the support and guidance of demonic influences, developed his human depravity to a level that would have enabled him to be as powerful and evil as he eventually became. This is not to discount his human culpability, as it requires a great amount of original depravity and a willful surrender to sinful nature to allow this kind of influence to take root and flourish within a human existence.

But, back to Marx...

We must consider if Marx was not only misguided, confused or even humanly depraved but also directly influenced by a/many demonic influence(s). And, as Mr. Breese may have attempted to illuminate with the sentence that began to collect this thought process for me, could that demon (or those demons) be openly and actively practicing even in this day and society that we are residing within? Is it (are they) whispering ever so subtly in the ear(s) of world leaders and an increasingly depraved society, speaking in tones once hushed but exponentially increasing in volume and vehemence?

As readers continue on through *Seven Men*, they must continue to consider the demonic influence leveled upon all seven of the men he highlights and how those men have been in the direct service of Satan and his minions. Perhaps we will not know the full truth of this hypothesis while I yet live in this physical realm.

Regardless, this chapter provided a series of points to depict the errors of a Marxist philosophy. There were four specific section listed and discussed. I found nothing in these sections that I would disagree with or find question regarding.

One very interesting bit that I found to be once again almost "prophetic" (that is, in an intellectual sense) was the rising star of liberation theology.

While doing some research on this topic a few years ago, I had come across an article which provided what I thought was an enlightening summarization of the history of the philosophy (and which briefly explains the most pressing concern of the movement, the destruction of the respect of the Holy Word of God):

"Throughout the 1960s, the major topic dominating the theological scene was secularization of the Gospel. Paul van Buren, author of The Secular Meaning of the Gospel, declared that the modern Christian must be a secular person with a secular understanding of existence. In other words, the world should dictate the content of the Christian message. With a secular savior, a secular mission, and a secular future, it was a short step to the "God-is-dead" theology of the later 1960s.

Then with a troublesome God out of the way, it was time to usher in Marx. So-called "theologians of hope," like Jurgen Moltmann, called for a new understanding of the Kingdom of God where the future is shaped by the actions of men rather than the sovereignty of God.

Theologians from Protestant, Catholic, and Jewish ranks have embraced Liberation Theology as the answer for a secular society. While they vary in the degree to which they espouse Marxist ideology or in the religious terminology they employ, all liberation theologians share one common ground: They abandon some or all of their traditional, orthodox teaching. Perhaps most frightening, many young theologians are never exposed to any substantive theology in which God and the Scriptures still reign as absolute." -- Bill McIlhany (Liberation Theology on the Move in the United States)

In specific, Mr. Breese's reference to his 1960's conference visit to the Vatican was most intriguing. During this visit he started to see the groundwork being laid for a combination of Marxism and Christianity. At the time, he saw no possible way to have that transition ever consummated. However, it did not take long for him to change his mind about the possible influence of the movement.

The interested and engaged reader will also find it to be illuminating that he credited the roots of this movement to the Catholic Church and that Latin American countries provide a stronghold for those who adhere to that movement. There is no possible way that Mr. Breese could have seen the ascendency of Jorge Mario Bergoglio, known today as Pope Francis, the leader of the modern day Catholic church.

The statements and publicly demonstrated viewpoint of Pope Francis clearly solidifies the comments of Breese in this context and prove to be almost eerie in its accuracy.

Overall, as Breese comments, Marxism moves across the world in many a strange disguise and I do not doubt that Dave Breese himself would be somewhat surprised – in hindsight – at the accuracy/validity of this statement.

CHAPTER 6

Chapter six of *Seven Men* introduces us to the figure of Julius Wellhausen and his impact on the theology of the Christian church from the middle of the 19th century to modern times.

Julius Wellhausen may very well be the most influential person in the active destruction of the basic, fundamental doctrines of the Christian church. With the compiling and provision of his theological thoughts as handed to society, we see Christianity proverbially jumping from the frying pan into the fire. This surrender of fundamentals of the faith may have been the greatest personal triumph of Satan and was undoubtedly a dearly won victory for the cause of evil.

Wellhausen was a very important component of the promotion of historical (or "higher") criticism. And, through his flawed view of God and His Holy Word, we have seen the demise of the respect that is supernaturally demanded. Wellhausen took the fledgling thoughts of evolution as provided through Darwin and Marx and applied those concepts to what is considered by many to be a "superior" form of Biblical understanding & appreciation.

With his developed philosophy we see the complete undermining of the veracity and power of the Word as considered by the masses of humanity. He challenged the fact that the Word of God was divinely inspired and that God Himself had provided it to mankind in an originally perfect form/condition. Instead, Wellhausen (and, subsequently all higher criticism proponents) focused on proving the academic beginnings of the Bible, attempting to "prove" that the Bible had largely (or in some higher critics opinion, entirely) been provided to man by man without any direct influence or control by God.

As a direct result of this change of perception of the Holy and true Word (and the turning of the back on sola scriptura, even by those mainstream reformation Protestant congregations that once relied wholly upon the sola scriptura perspective) inspired (and given solely) by God through mankind to provide for the edification and instruction of mankind (2 Tim 3:16, 17), we have abandoned the necessary humility of the factual position of every member of mankind. We have exchanged the truth of God for a lie (Romans 1:25). Instead of admitting our irreconcilable faults and the absolute truths of the Word due to our reverence for God and submission to Him we can now, by generated intellectual criticism, attribute the creation of essentially any portion of Scripture to a primitive and backwards human author. Once that has been accomplished, we can then discredit any portion of Scripture we may wish to discredit and do so in the pursuit of "truth", "liberty", "social progress" and "academic recognition". After all, isn't the adage, "Heck, nobody's perfect" applicable here? Why consider the writings of the Bible any more valid, reasonable or steadfast if they came solely from man to man? Maybe the original writers made a mistake, or perhaps other alterations were made over time to corrupt the meaning as originally intended by the primitive author?

Wellhausen was not alone in his desire to change society's traditional Biblical viewpoint. However, he was the most vital of the final finishing touches of such a thought process and it is upon his legacy that so much theological error exists and is running rampant in our modern era, compounding error at every turn.

It seems almost humorous to consider a Christian church or individual "Christian" who would willingly vacate the supernatural authority of the Word of God. For, doing so eliminates any perceived true supernatural requirements for following the instruction of that literary authority. Sadly, not only is this thought process the exact opposite of humorous, it is that which provides the basis of many "believers" in our current society.

Ultimately, we find ourselves making void (in current society, not in actual reality) the commandments and values of God. Especially through the Bultmannism that is so prevalent in our theologians today. They teach their congregations/students in the same methods and philosophies today and heap error upon error while sowing the seeds of discontent and disrespect. Our mighty God (whose longsuffering is to be absolutely praised!) is daily lectured to via conceited and ignorant talking heads. Those who would rather choose to pay no attention to His glorious everlasting Word openly mock the ways of the true Sovereign Creator God. All of this has been predicated upon the historical (or, "higher") criticism of the Bible.

There is no possible means that can be used to diminish the role of historical criticism in the destruction and disassembly of the true

Christian church today. If Wellhausen was hoping to eliminate the true doctrines of the Bible in practice throughout church fellowships around the world, he would no doubt be very pleased.

J. Gresham Machen, in his work *Christianity and Liberalism* provides us with some key thoughts in this discussion that I found particularly valuable (as presented on pages 97 & 98 of *Seven Men*), not the least of which clearly demonstrates a modern symptom of the schizophrenia of Christianity:

"The rise of this modern naturalistic liberalism has not come by chance, but has been occasioned by important changes which have recently taken place in the conditions of life. The past one hundred years have witnessed the beginning of a new era in human history, which may conceivably be regretted, but certainly cannot be ignored, by the most obstinate conservatism. The change is not something that lies beneath the surface and might be visible only to the discerning eye; on the contrary it forces itself upon the attention of the plain man at a hundred points. Modern inventions and the industrialism that has been built upon them have given us in many respects a new world to live in; we can no more remove ourselves from that world than we can escape from the atmosphere that we breathe."

Machen, J. Gresham (2011-10-18). Christianity and Liberalism (Kindle Locations 46-51). Fig. Kindle Edition.

What we see increasingly developing in rapidity, influence and scope in our modern age is the contempt and scorn of Biblical foundational truths. It is due to the widely held desires and beliefs of our academia-worshiping world driven to wide success by those with "itching ears" (2 Tim 4:3). Whether termed "progress", "scientific" or "educational", humanity is clearly most interested in embracing humanism and denying the Lord.

Sadly, the destruction and disdain of the Word is not isolated solely to non-Christian demographic groups. Instead, we see a Para-Christian type of belief system also being fostered and formed. This Para-Christian worldview is subtle and incorporates much of the language saved for traditional Biblically based Christianity (and the language connection is vital for the health and well being of this Satan-Human strategy). It is being developed intentionally to replace (through the 100 points Machen describes above, in conjunction with the common language connection and the support of the modern clergy) the traditional Christianity that once held God in such a position of ultimate respect and appreciation. In place of the traditional God-fearing Christianity of true belief in the one Sovereign Creator God with reverence, proper respect and complete dedication to the triune God, we now have a "Christianity" that subjects their version of "god" to a position inferior to the power of collaborative humanity.

This new type of Para-Christianity is running rampant throughout all demographic groups, in all cities and across the globe. It has infected and affected essentially every church in the United States and beyond. It has done this through both the will of the people (itching ears) and the teaching in most modern seminary environments.

In my compilation of this book, I attempted to find any source to credit with a listing of seminaries teaching the Bible in light of historical ("higher") criticism. Sadly, I could find no definitive listing available, likely due to the fact that the method is so widely in use coupled to the lack of understanding between the two methods. However, a book by Dale Martin entitled *Pedagogy of the Bible: An Analysis and Proposal* does list the following six points that definitively isolate the conditions of the modern seminary environment:

1. Historical criticism of one type or another is the dominant foundational method taught to theological students (esp. in conservative schools!).

2. Most students are not being taught to think critically about textuality and interpretation in general.

3. Students are not being taught theological hermeneutics sufficiently, meaning that they are less likely to function as well-equipped guides for teaching responsible and creative theological interpretation of the Bible in their own religious communities.

4. Students entering seminary/colleges lack Bible knowledge and the ability to think theologically.

5. Students are not being helped enough to integrate the different disciplines learned in a typical ministerial education, i.e. too much compartmentalization.

6. The modern theological school is not doing enough to help train church leaders to interpret the Bible in creative, imaginative, and theologically sophisticated ways.

The failure of our seminaries to properly teach or reinforce accurate and reverent Biblical principals has directly led to the destruction of the institution known as the God-fearing church fellowship. Now we do not attempt to eliminate inaccurate teachings or false doctrines, we search for any church that gets as much correct as is possible. Fundamentalism is confused with evangelism. Evangelism is substituted as an example of functional and perhaps even thriving Christianity. It is the example given for the modern pinnacle of Christian Spirituality. However, evangelism has been shown (through the glass of history) to barter or parley away fundamentals of the faith to gain "ecumenism" and "mutual respect" or "understanding", no matter what the spiritual cost. Is there any way to deny the direct demonic involvement in the actions establishing the spread of higher criticism?

With the rise of this Para-Christianity (liberalism) based upon the failures of historical criticism, we will not see a widespread return to traditional and true Christianity. For, the people have taken the flavor of this new version of "Christianity" and like the taste too much to turn away from it now. And, as Breese writes, the liberalist version of Christianity will exist as a parasite inside of the true church. Also like any parasite, it will cause (and, in fact, is actively causing even now) the suffering and dwindling of the host.

The powers entrusted solely to the true church of God will continue to exist only within that body, the parasite will never demonstrate the benefits of the true powers. The new liberalist Christianity may attempt to grasp the values of the traditional true church, but it will be a failure at every turn. They may report successes, but they are partial, relative and empty when compared to those provided by the Holy Spirit indwelt believing body. There will be no true refuge found in the halls of the new Christianity, there will be no truly redeeming values, there will be no eternal reward or superior purpose. For, those refuges, those values, those rewards and that superior God-given purpose is found only within the true church.

As Machen goes on to write in Christianity and Liberalism:

"Is there no refuge from strife? Is there no place of refreshing where a man can prepare for the battle of life? Is there no place where two or three can gather in Jesus' name, to forget for the moment all those things that divide nation from nation and race from race, to forget human pride, to forget the passions of war, to forget the puzzling problems of industrial strife, and to unite in overflowing gratitude at the foot of the Cross? If there be such a place, then that is the house of God and that the gate of heaven. And from under the threshold of that house will go forth a river that will revive the weary world."

Machen, J. Gresham (2011-10-18). Christianity and Liberalism (Kindle Locations 2307-2311). Fig. Kindle Edition.

May those of us in the truth of Jesus and in His awesome Body by grace through faith alone continue to pray that we might make a temporary refuge and guide people into the ways of Christ, our eternal King and only Messiah!

CHAPTER 7

The next chapter in *Seven Men* describes the effect, however unintentional the range of scope, that Albert Einstein has had on the course of history and how that is reflected in society today.

Before reading *Seven Men* I had not considered that Albert Einstein could be included in this book. Upon seeing the basic premise and presentation of the chapter come to its conclusion, we are lead to feel somewhat sympathetic to the life plight of one of the greatest scientific minds ever recognized.

At its core, the life of Albert Einstein was probably spent in an almost constant awe of nature and his surroundings. I could not consider any motivation for the quantity/quality of thought that Einstein first developed and then provided to the world should creation's awesome splendor not been a significant contributor. For some individuals, the pursuit of truth is the paramount purpose of life. However, the pursuit of truth can take many forms based upon the passion that lies within the human psyche. In the case of Albert Einstein, his life purpose through knowledge was insatiable and he felt propelled to continue observing and revealing truths of the natural world.

A different pursuit of humanity often takes the form of re-evaluating history based upon current events. Something that we, as human beings often do, is attempt to determine motivations and justifications for world events in history past. Through the hindsight microscope, people attempt to press certain political or ethical viewpoints to the point of acceptance, twisting and manipulating facts as they go. Few things have caused more tumult in the minds and philosophies of this world than has the discovery and development of nuclear energy principles. Albert Einstein was essential in the pursuit of those principles, though his consideration of the science preceding the development of nuclear energy did not take the form of weaponization. No doubt his pathway of thought was focused upon more intrinsic and innocent pathways.

Some may think it funny or odd that such a bright individual with so much capability of thought would not have considered the entire process of nuclear science research to the point of the twisting of said scientific principles to becoming the most destructive weapon ever developed (and, therefore, the most politically influential military component ever). Principles that Einstein first chased about in his mind, there on a chalkboard in his lab, and then demonstrated to others were meant to propose/explain the functionality of parts of the creation model. From these innocent and simplistic beginnings came an eventual chain reaction of destruction that would have far reaching implications in the future of humanity. From the chalkboard to the battlefield and subsequently into the horrified mind of every person in the developed world, in less time than it took for one man to live a complete adult human life, man was "empowered" with the weapons to destroy the entire world.

The theory of relativity issue presented and developed in this chapter is another example of the ability and inclination of an increasingly depraved humanity to alter the basic facts of a situation. They do this to press a certain thought process or philosophy upon others in a means of both undermining God and wielding the ultimate control possible upon their peers. For some, it is not manifested as a world domination type of control, for their minds and motivations are too crude and simplistic for those pursuits. For them, it may be a means of appearing intelligent to others, trying to manipulate friends, family, coworkers, etc. into believing that a certain individual is more intelligent than they may very well be, inspiring some sort of respect. For others it is the fad of the time, something everyone is doing and thinking. It is so very sad that such basic scientific principles can be, once again, twisted by a depraved mind.

So began the "snowballing" of his philosophy/understanding that, at its core, was a scientific and intellectual diamond. But, that diamond was quickly hidden by the "snow" of the ignorance, short-mindedness, and the depravity of man to the detriment of the true value of the principles. We took something wonderful that could have been so truly valuable to the enlightenment and recognition of the power of God in the minds of the world and we dumbed it down to mean nothing of the size and scope it could begin to inspire. We, in essence, reduced it to the lowest possible common denominator.

Ultimately, although Einstein could not have foreseen the misunderstanding of his theory of relativity in the minds of man, he did his best to attempt to correct the failings of humanity in this regard. However, as was proven by the world in regard to his nuclear principles, that which humanity wishes to twist to its short-minded advantage it twists to the fullest possible extent. Einstein could not have stopped the flawed adoption and destruction of his great thoughts.

Humanity is not averse to "spitting into the wind" in its attempt to flex the depravity and will of the majority of its members. Natural laws exist outside of the power of mankind to wholly control. This is the case in every respect, in every avenue of nature and science. However, one of the most amazing manifestations of human depravity includes the ability for mankind to practice a form of increasing megalomania, which makes them believe that nature itself will one day be at their every beck and call (for more on this subject, read *The Abolition of Man* by C.S. Lewis). From homosexuality to nuclear holocaust, from abortion to one world government, humanity believes they have it all figured out or shortly will do so (and that is the most simple definition of humanism). Meanwhile, self-government continues to degrade in essentially all members of society and is being replaced by great arcs of government power and control.

I wonder at the potential thoughts/science Einstein may have had but became convinced that sharing them or even partially displaying them would create more turmoil by an increasingly depraved humanity. How great was the true scope of some of his thoughts? Did he consider them all to the point of substantial development, ready for presentation to mankind or did he intentionally choose to keep them to himself to prohibit another manipulation of basic facts of nature to the selfish and self-delusional short-term benefits of a depraved humanity?

I believe that we can take the principles of the life of Albert Einstein and the unintentional effects of his thought processes and apply it to our own lives. It will teach us about a great thinker, it will teach us about humanity as a whole, it will teach us something of ourselves regarding our own propensity to manipulate when we do not work in accordance with the Word and the Spirit.

CHAPTER 8

This chapter in *Seven Men* covers the multi-faceted influence that Sigmund Freud has had on culture and an increasingly willing society.

It is likely impossible to get all readers to agree on which of the seven people covered in this book is the most depraved of the group. Instead, perhaps it is best to think of the individuals presented and discussed thus far as a puzzle, each one fitting into the ideal place to provide an image of the heart and soul of the enemy of our Sovereign Creator God. These seven men alone may not provide the only puzzle pieces that mankind will be given, which is something only time will tell (one day humanity might very well see a volume entitled *Nine Men Who Rule From The Grave*, for example). However, there is little doubt in my mind that any one of those in *Seven Men* was quite as versatile in their impact on society and the current culture as was (and continues to be) Sigmund Freud.

While Freud required the actions of the others we have previously covered in order for him to rise to a point of incredible influence and effective encouragement of depravity, he made the pursuit of increasing depravity a sort of art form in various methods and medias. Freud, for all of his failings and obvious blunders, captured the attention of the common man and did so in astounding fashion, forever tainting the relative morality of the masses beyond that which will be repaired prior to the obliteration of sin and the engineers of said sin by our Heavenly Father.

Freud, who was actually found to be intellectually wanting in many respects (both by his contemporaries and by historians since), was more than capable of recognizing the fact that he had his own fears, how those fears affected him and how he could then use those same emotional and psychological motivating factors/tendencies to manipulate others. In addition, there is little doubt that he was highly motivated to normalize his own depravities by trying to make them appear normal in the lives of all of the people he interacted with.

Freud stumbled from one psychological blunder to another throughout the course of his professional existence. From hypnotism, the early stages of regressive therapy, psychoanalysis and free association, he touched upon whatever seemed like a good idea at the time. Instead of utilizing a specific systematic method to his "medicine" and "practice" thereof, the man jumped mentally about without consistency or apparent actual honest purpose.

Freud's true power in persuasion was his self-confident nature that allowed him to appear (and, perhaps, to actually be) completely confident of his philosophies, methods and motivations, regardless of the functionality or ability to independently judge the success of those methods and motivations.

One of the most effective methods of Satan revolves around his ability to project multiple fronts, organizations and methods at one time. The various groups or philosophies may appear to be in competition to each other, allowing mankind to align themselves to a specific group which may promise to oppose evil or promote a type of morality. However, all of these groups, methods and motivations under the origin of anything other than God and His perfect plan as outlined in His Word are doomed to be but tools of Satan in the fullness of time. Society may not be able to identify this (or even truly be interested in the debate or concern at all) and that is the ultimate hope of Satan.

Such were the philosophies and ramblings of Sigmund Freud. He created a means by which he could describe and attribute the actions of mankind and he did so in a way that has manifested itself in various ways in the decades that have passed since his death. But, all of those ways are multi-faceted, convoluted, and without truth. In addition, all of those ways have distracted mankind from the truth of the Word, simple (while factual) explanations to the pressing questions of life, existence and purpose. These valuable answers have been replaced by philosophies and conjectures that have poisoned our culture and continue to lead an all too willing humanity to deny God and the offer of Christ to each one of us (and the responsibility that entails).

I hesitate to admit that I cannot imagine a world that existed prior to the establishment of the methods and philosophies of Freud. A world in which mankind still had some ability (perhaps even an inclination and trend) to recognize the true purpose of life. Instead, Freud changed everything related to the human psyche at its most basic level, altering the mentality of humanity and planting the seeds of our currently flourishing hedonistic, sexually driven society.

One does not need to look long to see the far-reaching implications of his foolish philosophies. Just look at the top 40 pop charts, Hollywood, Nashville, even local schools with their increasing sexting and underage sexual deviance or the sexual improprieties of the modern Christian clergy and standard household family members. The fascination with the sexual part of the human existence is foremost on the minds of society.

The masses focus their lives on their hollow, empty pursuits. They work endlessly, toiling away at increasing their worldly education; they neglect their families for their careers. They invest uncountable dollars on hobbies and empty pursuits. All the while, they ignore God and pretend to not know of Him and His ways (Romans 1:18-21). Freud fostered the thought of determination and developed the psychological basis that mankind needed to run morally rampant. In this way we see that Freud, although the author of this depraved train of thought, was not the sole purchaser of the product. Far from it, the masses slowly accepted and eventually embraced that false bill of goods he was selling.

Only a devotion to the Lord and the truth of His Word can really point out the obvious answers to the common questions all of mankind have. Freud tried to engineer valid responses that would replace those truths that God clearly provided for in His Holy Word for all to see who would accept said truth. Freud tried to usurp the sole truth that can easily answer the questions of why we exist and why we act as we do. Those answers are provided for anyone to accept should they truly wish to do so with humility and thankfulness. Instead, we learn that mankind is far more likely to be inclined to deny these truths in the pursuit of something devious and diabolical:

"Therefore God also gave them up to uncleanness, in the lusts of their hearts, to dishonor their bodies among themselves, who exchanged the truth of God for the lie, and worshiped and served the creature rather than the Creator, who is blessed forever. Amen." Romans 1:24, 25, NKJV.

CHAPTER 9

Chapter nine of *Seven Men* covers the absolutely pervasive and overwhelming influence that John Dewey has had on our increasingly depraved society through the hearts, minds and souls of our children.

In the previous chapter, which discussed the thoughts, philosophies and actions of Sigmund Freud, I postulated that no one person found in *Seven Men* might be considered superior in the process of eliminating God. Many forces and individuals are responsible for eventually eliminating most eternally useful transcendent thought in the minds of man and ensuring the destruction of our Christian nation (the United States of America), allowing for the "fundamental transformation of America" as promoted by U.S. President Barack Obama in 2008.

However, one man can be credited with the most influential change to our society, far before 2008, creating an environment in which the humanist inclined, God denying public would be enabled to function effectively as indoctrinated members of a Godless society. Without question, this one man takes the solid and obvious form as the figurehead leader of a most insidious method of control and persuasion.

That man was John Dewey.

Upon completing this chapter from Breese, the reader is convinced that there can be no more active and subversive method of spreading the "values" of secular humanism (and, therefore, the flawed thought process and inferior morals of the philosophies of Satan) than the public education system. Whether, at the time, Dewey was aware or convinced of his full capability in this regard or not, he slammed the accelerator to the floor and actively drove the vehicle called "Exceptional America" over the cliff into embraced depravity & ultimately into the very lake of fire.

A nation cannot be "religious", as a nation is geographically or politically defined. However, the people of that land can have a predominant spiritual thought process. At one time, the predominant thought process of those citizens of the United States of America were essentially Christian from the standpoint of accepting two obvious universal truths:

1) Creator God is the Sovereign reality.

2) You will be held responsible to Him, eventually.

With these facts laid as a burden of social/self responsibility upon the mind and soul of most American children, our nation prospered. As those two basic spiritual tenants were removed and replaced by humanistic values, we can see a direct correlation to every possible negative attribute of living the human life.

John Dewey singlehandedly led the way to the most pervasively possible means of eliminating God from the minds of our nation's future and he did so with only one hope: doing so with increasing efficiency and effectiveness. Yes, others (including Satan and his minions) surely desired the immediate removal of Christianity from every aspect of personal and social life in America. However, Dewey had the power, the capability and the desire to make this eventually occur on an increasingly rapid scale and to make the finished result appear so natural for all involved directly within it.

I am a bit like our Apostle Paul was. As he was both Jew and Roman, I was both public and home schooled. The first seven grades of my education occurred in the realm of the dusty, aging halls of rural western America public schools. Eventually, upon our conversion to Christianity and fellowship with other believers in the Body, my parents chose to remove me from public education and begin a home education. In this way I am well qualified to speak on behalf of both methods of instruction and compare the life of a boy (myself) both in unbelief, surrounded by the methods of blasphemous instruction as well as in belief while being "deprogrammed" and more classically trained. I also worked in the public education system as for almost seven years. I was often exposed to God defying curriculum, technology, conversation (conversation both amongst the staff and the students) and philosophy. I have been on the front lines of this battle both as a child and as an adult.

I can personally attest to the fact that the fallacy and pervasive destruction we call "public education" far exceeds even our grandest imagination (into the unseeable realm of the principalities and powers). And, essentially all parents everywhere (both Christian and secular) would not give a second thought as to where their tender and impressionable young children are at for 7+ hours a day, nor what they are really being taught. Parents assume that, since public school eventually provided them with a basis to live a fairly normal everyday routine life, that it is also good enough for their children. What many people do not understand (either through active action (endorsement or selfishness) or passivity (laziness or carelessness)) is that the humanist teachings in the public school system are growing greater in strength, subtler in presentation and more credible when viewed by an increasingly depraved society.

As a result, children are truly being indoctrinated in classrooms across America and the world. That indoctrination, no different than the Hitler Youth camps of World War II, is actively pursued (and assumed) today to control and manipulate minds to accept humanism and denounce true Spirituality. John Dewey and his league of henchmen first envisioned this opportunity and began to emotionally and intellectually exploit children with the intent to create super-humanists who will one day usher in their perfect Godless utopian age. They have succeeded in creating the life force to reach this goal.

Dewey did not act alone in this period. He was accompanied and assisted by a handful of his contemporaries who were considered (and, amongst many in society are still considered to this day) intellectual giants in the race of humanity. The names are more or less familiar; Albert Einstein, Charles F. Potter, Thomas Mann and Julian Huxley were but a few. These men (as well as John Dewey) all served as directors and board members of the society called the First Humanist Society of New York, founded in 1929. All of the before mentioned individuals assisted in creating the basis of what is known within the last 100 years as humanism, they were in at the ground level so-to-speak. Dewey, Potter and Einstein also signed the original Humanist Manifesto (also commonly referred to as Humanist Manifesto I) in 1933 (see Appendix A for full text).

We have already discussed and developed the thoughts of Einstein so I will not touch upon him further. Mann won a Nobel Prize for his contribution to literature. Some of his books encouraged inappropriate bisexual relationships including those shared between adult men and children while several other of his books pressed forward his thoughts on utopian humanism. Huxley was a British eugenicist and evolutionary biologist as well as the first director of

UNESCO. Potter was a Unitarian minister. It is Potter himself who wrote:

"Education is thus a most powerful ally of humanism, and every American school is a school of humanism. What can a theistic Sunday school's meeting for an hour once a week and teaching only a fraction of the children do to stem the tide of the five-day program of humanistic teaching?" (Charles F. Potter, "Humanism: A New Religion," 1930)

It is obvious that public education has long been used to further the cause of humanism. Humanism is a program in which Satan can throw his full support, authorization and sanction behind.

Public education has been created to manipulate the children of the public and alter their actions both as children and as eventual functional illiterates. However, the purpose of the manipulation of facts is not solely based in the desire to provide a certain set of supposedly accurate information (which are - in truth - lies) and humanist "values". It is to create an environment of control and submissiveness in all realms of the human life and to make that environment increasingly pervasive and "natural". This is the true will of Satan and has been for countless years. Enslaving humanity to his will and eventual destiny is the only long-term purpose of Satan. Humanism falls completely within the trap of Satan and has no hope of ever escaping. Public education is intentionally creating humanistic children and altering the power structures and influences of the traditional means of control and education of children, namely, the two parent family unit.

Listed below are a few of the quickly considered representative examples of the various powers of the school system being wielded against the children and families that they are claiming control over (and there are dozens of new examples daily):

1) Some schools are actively screening home provided lunch food choices sent with students by the parents of these children and throwing away whatever items the school might find "unacceptable". (http://www.carolinajournal.com/exclusives/display_exclusive.html?i d=8762)

2) Recently, a 5 year old child in Florida was first ridiculed and eventually prohibited from saying a prayer prior to eating her lunch

by a school staff or faculty member (the school denies this has occurred and has refused to identify the actual people involved). (http://www.washingtontimes.com/news/2014/apr/2/florida-kindergartner-says-teacher-told-her-youre-/)

3) A sixth grade student in California was repeatedly forced to wrongly admit culpability by school officials for handing out intelligent design acknowledging paperwork to friends at her school. After her numerous humiliating experiences with school administration, she was advised to cease and desist all future person-to-person discussion on any subject questioning facets/aspects of school curriculum. (http://www.news10.net/story/news/local/roseville/2014/11/18/religio us-flyer-in-school-leads-to-legal-dispute/19208685/)

In spite of these facts and their overwhelming numbers of public supporters of this increased control and power, some individuals have stood against this and continue to do so.

Mr. Breese, for example is one of those who tried to warn the world about the dangers of the public education system. Who else could he have included in the chapter on Dewey but J Grescham Machen? Machen's book, first printed in 1924, seems to exactly (and repeatedly) predict the future of America in many respects. Breese, 65 years later (1990), chose not to go so far as to claim all hope lost in the pursuit of halting the power of a humanistic public education system but did indicate that the final seconds of the clock were ticking in our society and that something had to be done immediately or risk losing our capability to communicate Christianity completely (or exist via the truths of the Bible in any capacity). Sadly, Breese had his book published prior to the explosion of the internet which has only served to more widely and effectively spread humanism and the methods of the public education system (see chapter 13 of this companion), establishing public instruction as the only means of legal education in an increasing number of places. Parents, at one point, had the option to homeschool children. That opportunity is eroding daily and will eventually be outlawed in America as it has been in other countries around the world (supposedly outlawed in the best interest of society).

Another voice speaking out about the dangers of the public education system (though perhaps not to the fullest possible aspect of actively identifying Satan) is Charlotte Thomson Iserbyt (author of, amongst other volumes, *The Deliberate Dumbing Down of America*). She has characterized those in our society pressing forward with socialism, communism and humanism as "change agents". Undoubtedly, the message against public education is still available and is beyond reproach. However, this information is ignored, boycotted and willfully neglected by essentially all of the global society.

And, that is where I come to the true problem. The masses have embraced the humanist philosophy and they are increasingly addicted to those philosophies that they have easy access to. Dewey may have been the image of the man who began the fullest possible exploitation of children in our nation, but he is only a representation of a greater horror.

Sadly, the fallacies of public education have continued for so long and have been propogated so widely that many simple and basic truths have become occluded or even completely hidden from plain sight (the truth can be obscured from view but can never be defeated or extinguished). I will quickly touch upon the subject of the age old debated phrase; "The separation of church and state." and it's various incarnations.

There is no constitutional language, nor any language in any original American constitutional law allowing for such phrasing to be used and considered as the "law of the land". Thomas Jefferson actively participated in the crafting of the U.S. Constitution, though he was not the sole author. However, several supreme court rulings (beginning with Reynolds v. U.S., 98 U.S. 145 (1878)) determined the non-contextually derived opinion of Jefferson upon the proper roles of church and state in private correspondence to supercede constitutional precedent and law while also interpreting his feelings upon the entire subject posthumously (and, as mentioned before, long after his death). Sadly, they did not consider the true intent of his spiritual mentors and contemporaries, which played a key role upon his apparent thought regarding tha matter, nor the full context and weight of his writings.

Upon a close inspection of all available facts, the founding fathers (including Thomas Jefferson) clearly did not find it reasonable for the government to SANCTION RELIGIOUS ORDERS AND BODIES. They could plainly see that the government should not meddle in the affairs of the Church (various denominations of

Christian faith). Nor did they see any room for government to officially support any state or federal adoption of a specific Christian religious group/denomination (i.e., Baptists, Presbyterians, Methodists, Lutherans, etc.). The founding fathers (by-and-large) obviously represented many Christian denominations and did clearly recognize the existence of One True Creator God. Those founding fathers also recognized the need to prohibit one Christian denomination from burdening or unduly influencing the federal government. They did not attempt to provide for the exclusivity of Christianity from the minds and hearts of the people who both serve and are served by the government. Nor did they see any reason to provide guidance as such in any adopted government documents or legislation.

If there was to be any meaning conveyed from their private correspondence (and noticeably absent from officially adopted use by the federal government), the preponderence of writing proves that the government is to be hands off of religion (which at that time was predominately Christian in basis) but does not indicate that Christian ideals, doctrines, ethics or involvement of the Christian faith could not be freely practised in any specific government buildings or by government employees in any venue.

As such, a person would be wise to recognize that the government cannot force a person to practice a certain religion or sect/denomination of any religion. However, this truth does not then provide for the natural necessity of the exclusion of any Christian worship or recognition in any government environment by individuals (and - in truth - as protected by the first amendment). In fact, one of the "growth pains" of our humanist (or "progressive") society revolves around what to base morality and ethics upon while separating those ethics from the original Christian roots of our historical founding (and based upon the Bible, a document that humanists despise and discredit). Our education system is an unending battlefield in the war pitting church versus state, family versus bureaucrat and soul versus Satan.

That terrifying truth is that our Godless society liked what it heard from Dewey and his associates. They did not reject it or tar and feather the satanic philosophies and run the people supporting those philosophies out of town. Instead, society was deceived and intrigued. They embraced with increasing rapidity that which usurps God, the cause of Christ and the Holy Word. They actively exchanged the truth of God for a lie. That is why it will not be stopped by humanity. It will amplify itself until God Himself stretches out His hand and stops the evil of Satan once and for all. And, until then, humanity will find little or no solid ethical ground to stand upon now that they have gone to great lengths to erode the stable truth of morality as provided by the author of morality: God.

The decline of every society of this world (including the United States of America) is directly related to the decline of the self-government of humanity, the increasing rarity of human's personal responsibilities, and the general human desire to ignore any repercussions regarding their personal failures.

All of these ills can be attributed to the seemingly inevitable weakening of our morality due to the replacement of our true Sovereign Creator God with the increasing "value" of humanism:

Humanism is, at best, a shattered mirror desperately attempting to accurately reproduce and reflect the original perfect plan of the one true and Sovereign God. At times, a small shard of the shattered mirror of humanism may chance to reflect a tiny piece of the true image of morality originally instituted by God.

However, on the whole, the shattered collection of pieces will give the viewer a distorted, disfigured and destroyed picture. A reflection that will not, in fact cannot, accurately represent reality.

Eventually, history will prove that humanism will have failed to even remotely approach the vaunted peak that it was designed to climb; that satanic precipice designed to provide the illusion of substantiated morality superior to the only truly righteous morality as solely implemented with such love, grace, beauty and effortless power by the one Sovereign Creator God. And the culmination of that love and morality was demonstrated perfectly through the life and death of Jesus Christ and our completed Word of God.

CHAPTER 10

The tenth chapter in *Seven Men* provides an insightful look at the bearing John Maynard Keynes played upon the global economic system and how that has set in place another stone of the foundation providing for the world playing as God.

Economics is really something that many people do not understand even in part, not to mention completely. So it was of little surprise to me that, of the people I spoke to when compiling this book, none could tell me what Keynesian economics really was, or what its role is in the global government program. I was also (and must contend still relatively am) incomplete in my knowledge and thought process considering Keynes and his economic system. However, Dave Breese provided a solid base to begin to really consider the ramifications of the basic components of Keynesian economics.

I have been considering why people do not understand or even attempt to understand economics. It seems to be a relatively wise intellectual pursuit in our present societal system. How could one ever truly hope to be financially successful (that is, capable of being "relatively" financially secure) unless one either stumbles blindly into so much money that they cannot improperly squander it in their lifetime, or, one has properly planned an effective strategy to use economics to their financial advantage.

Perhaps it is rooted in the fact that mankind – by and large – despises and loathes mathematics. People are generally completely intimidated by numbers as well as the functions necessary to grasp the full meaning of those numbers. Numbers surround us all every day but most people do not even begin to hope to gain anything more than a day-by-day survival type of acknowledgement and functionality with those numbers.

Perhaps it is, upon gaining a familiarity with mathematics and basic economics, others become aware of the short-term nature inherently required in all economic systems of thought. This might make some feel insecure in their ability to become, or stay, relatively financially secure.

Whatever the cause, mankind spends little time studying economics and are therefore largely at the mercy of both those who do have a superior understanding of economics and the government, which has chosen to play "god" with the financial system as allowed & empowered in our increasingly globalized society. The past 80 years of economic progression have increasingly shown that a Keynesian economic system is the choice of the United States government. There is little hope that the government will deviate from this course in a future time, unless it is made necessary/convenient by the complete adoption of first a socialist system and, eventually, a communist form of government.

Keynesian economics can be summed up in two basic statements. First, that short-term economic philosophy is really all that can be foreseen and is all that really matters. Second, that the government must be relied upon to provide economic stimulus.

John Maynard Keynes did not care about long-term economic planning or policies (unless they directly competed with his short-term goals). He has been quoted numerous times referring to the deferment of future economic concerns due to present economic policy. And, he is famously quoted as having rejected long-term considerations by proposing that, in the long-term, "we are all dead". Yet, Americans seem content to allow his system of economic philosophy to create (and dictate) the daily lifecycle both themselves and their descendants (children/grandchildren, etc.) are financial slaves to.

John Maynard Keynes believed that the perfect panacea for economic difficulties existed solely in the "major responsibility" of government, that is, that government was solely responsible for - and capable of - solving any economic difficulties by creating the financial capability and impetus necessary to resolve all financial challenges. What this has created in a fairly short amount of time is dependence by the people upon the government to take charge of the economic situation, no matter the event.

Regulation really equates to control. It is the government choosing the field of play, the objective of the game, the rules of said game and, when down late in the game, they change the rules to their liking and advantage. In an imperfect world populated by individuals who operate with an intrinsic sin nature (and exploitive mindset), some regulation proves necessary to support "civilization". However, we have moved beyond necessary regulations to game changing rule making by a system of government that is insistent upon winning (their definition at the time of decision), no matter what the cost. And, as Mr. Breese points out at the end of chapter 10 (and I have previously mentioned about others in this book), it is not really the fault of Keynes alone, it is also the fault of a lazy and increasingly depraved society that the government is put into a position to ever play "god", a role a size increasing government will always yearn to amplify and control.

In the long-term scheme of things, Keynes provided the philosophy and opportunity to allow the government to justify the globalization of the economic system. It is the people who allowed it to actually occur, for whatever reason they may have had. Sadly, the people do not understand why items are priced $4.99 in comparison to $5, not to mention how millions of people should financially interact. People believe they are getting a good deal on their free smartphone, or that they outsmarted the company when they "talked" down the dealership on their new car lease. They are also the ones who, for better or worse, choose to allow the tangible value of the United States to plummet (and the dollar to do so accordingly). They do this to allow their short-term possession goals to become relatively achievable and with no long-term planning, strategy or even considered & coherent thought. There was a time the people could have stopped this, but why do so when they do not understand it, have short-term goals and live financially day-to-day while trying to outdo their neighbors and co-workers?

Sadly, the long-term outlook as a result of this policy is increasing control by the globalized system and a greater control over all parts of life by the manifested governments of this world (not all of which are interested in the value/health of the United States and her citizens).

Behind the scenes lies Satan (Ephesians 6:12), actively controlling and closing his grip upon humanity, squeezing the spirit of life, the pursuit of the will of God and eternal salvation out of every person within his control (an ever growing number) while promising glory, power and riches to every man. However, mankind is not so foolish as to be incapable of realizing who wields the control, they simply choose to ignore the obvious fact.

CHAPTER 11

Chapter 11 of *Seven Men* directly exposes us to the basic thoughts and social impacts of existentialism and its first philosophical purveyor, Soren Kierkegaard.

I found this chapter to be both the least in-depth of the chapters and, in honor of its subject, the least satisfying. There seems to be difficulty present in the pursuit of defining existentialism. As so many have tried to greatly summarize the tenants and teachings of existentialism and have thus far failed, I find it very unlikely that I would suddenly stumble upon a valuable/successful means of paraphrasing or solidifying a more succinct and effective method myself. However, I will attempt to make it as simplistic as possible by identifying some basic components of existentialistic philosophy.

Existentialism cannot be considered outside of an individual's personal experience. It requires man to really identify his or her own experiences and how those experiences have impacted their life. In this way, they are both self-analyzing (to the point of self-absorption) and self-gratifying, seeking to improve their own environment (or existence) as it pleases them while also likely admitting that they will never truly reach a point where they can find ultimate utopia; which, strangely enough, is actually exactly what an existentialist wants. They do not want to reach a specific shared ultimate utopia, for life is about "the doing of the thing" and their personal response to that pursuit, not really achieving some greater social utopia as defined by society as a whole.

In this way, existentialism is truly – at its core - experiential. In other words, a practicing existentialist always considers himself or herself a work in progress through life experience, though they are alone capable of determining at what stage of progress/successful maturity they are at and are also therefore responsible only to themselves and their moral position to determine how that impacts themselves and the people around them. And, it is that process (which is perhaps concisely expressed as LIFE EXPERIENCE + SELF ANALYSIS + SELF-ACCEPTANCE OF INDIVIDUAL "STRENGTHS" / "WEAKNESSES" = UNIQUE LIFE

EXISTENCE) and their practice of that process that really is their rewarding purpose of life.

At the same time, a mature existentialist would deny that every person has the same desires, the same morality, the same spiritual components, the same possible God to serve. This, in part, is responsible for the displayed or apparent variances in definitions and philosophies of those considered to be under the umbrella of existentialism.

An existentialist's life is a bit like being suddenly and inexplicitly dropped into a 24 hour straight pinball machine tournament with thousands of others while there are no clearly defined rules, method of scoring or objectives. The only thing you really know is that as long as you attempt to compete you ensure your existence in this very moment. The little white ball bounces about hither, thither and yon. In the process, you must decide for yourself if you are doing well and try not to pay too much attention to the other competitors. Sometimes the machine makes noises and flashes lights, but you really don't know if that is a good thing or bad. Eventually, you either resign yourself to the recognition that you cannot ever be certain that you are competing well or you take joy in the fact that the rules, the scoring and the objectives don't matter to anyone other than yourself and you choose to embrace the experience as your reward.

Within the core being of essentially every human you will find a mind, soul and spirit making volitional choices about God, life, emotions and relationships with others. For many people, they feel nervous or hesitant about parts of their lives (for some, it may be every part of their life) and a great number of those in our midst wander through life wondering, "What is my purpose in this world"? Existentialism provides an answer to this question, or, put more accurately, a means to seemingly answer this question. Sadly, the answer can never be the correct one, but it does give people an opportunity to take false refuge in an incorrect answer (since any temporal answer that will distract them from the original question will likely suit them, if but in the short term).

For a person outside of a truly reconciled relationship with God and maturing in the Word of God, there is no genuine eternal hope or purpose that can be treasured day-by-day. This is usually reflected in sayings such as, "Anticipation is greater than realization.", and other related adages. Most existentialists feel insecure, unfulfilled, a bit socially lost or out of place emotionally. At least they do until they embrace their insecurities as the normal life experience for all of mankind (which is, sadly, a Satanic fallacy). In Christ, as our sole source of reconciliation to the Father, humanity has the capability to grasp eternal hope. Through the Word of God every man and woman can find life purpose and truth in regard to difficult life questions. Through existentialism, humanity can only delude themselves into eventually believing that they are on their own in a unique personal experience that no other will ever be able to truly and completely relate to which will likely end in nothing more than a natural physical death and that no eternal spiritual surety can be gained during their lifetime (and, for many existentialists, there is no eternity at all).

Kierkegaard is widely considered to be the first comprehensive proponent of existentialism and his philosophy is largely pointed to as the beginning of the existentialistic worldview. As agnostics believe it to be impossible to ever know God or really anything about God with any surety that can be completely relied upon, not to mention that true Godly knowledge could ever be passed successfully from one person to another, so too did Kierkegaard feel this way about the human psyche. His writings displayed this fact, as he chose to publish a series of books under different names and with different philosophical leanings all intended to culminate in the opportunity – should one ever happen to read all of his works – for the reader to even begin to conceptualize the process of existentialism. This did not really allow for one to grasp existentialism itself (as it is truly a unique experience for each individual) but provided the opportunity for one to begin to grasp the process of the existentialist life and life purposes. Since proper existentialism is solely possible in the unique manifestation of the existentialist's own life experience, Kierkegaard (as well as other existentialist philosophers) did not expect - or even really attempt - to provide life guidance or ethics that can be applied to every woman and/or man.

As a direct result, the isolated morality of an existentialist can perhaps be summarized thus:

If it feels good, do it - as long as it doesn't make another feel bad. But, don't ever do anything that makes you feel bad.

In this way we see that the motivation of an existentialist is ultimately self-centered while trying to prohibit activation of their guilty conscience for being too self-centered, too quickly.

Many people today use a hypocritical existentialist philosophy as their baseline for daily personal life objectives. They may say to their children "follow the golden rule" while they themselves consider "dog eat dog" to be the order of the day. The more forward thinking of these individuals may occasionally think about how their actions may affect others, but they are largely driven to do that which they wish to do as long as their guilty conscience is quelled. When it is not quelled, they do not consider God to be the cause of that or that a higher authority is the driver behind that persistent feeling. Instead, an existentialist claims that the guilty feeling is merely a manifestation of their personal life experience and that they will eventually overcome or embrace that feeling, making it something that improves their capability to deal with future life experiences. Many people use the expression, "That which doesn't kill us, makes us stronger." And, for many people, either consciously or unconsciously, they apply this mentality to their psyche directly as a means to an existentialistic end.

Kierkegaard postulated that it was possible to be both a Christian and an existentialist.

And, as I am unable to speak directly to the nature and state of his personal salvation, I can only use his writings and lifestyle as an example of his method of living a supposedly saved Christian life. I believe that he had a desire to seek God (though I am unable to truly determine his motivation for this seeking) but largely felt unable to do so effectively (in part due to his sub-conscious natural man deviation from the will of God and in part due to his lack of proper Biblical exposure with spiritually edifying fellowship). As a result, the life of Soren Kierkegaard was lived somewhat empty and he had a difficult time discovering the true purpose of life as he struggled to find a reason to find hope day to day. These variables all played into what became a philosophically tortured life culminating in a twisted mess of apparently contradictory writings.

The western United States has historically been a spiritual vacuum of a type allowing a convoluted mixture of paganism, cosmotheism, existentialism, and eastern mysticism to reside side by side with - and intertwined into - that which so many incorrectly call

"Christianity". As Christianity is the sole truly self-limiting moral belief system (due to the will/truth of the only Sovereign Creator God) while the other "spiritual" components all allow a person to live free of their inhibitions, an increasingly depraved humanity has decided to remove true Christianity (remember J. Grescham Machen's Liberal (or Para-) Christianity) from this spiritual tossed salad we call "religion". Existentialism has been a major component of this removal as it provides a method for self-analysis that usurps and undermines the will of God, replacing it with the will of mankind.

Whether Kierkegaard intended to create a replacement for Christianity or not is not really the issue. I do not believe he had a motivation to destroy Christianity. Instead, he appeared to struggle to communicate his thoughts on living. I find it almost impossible to avoid the fact that, deep within himself, Kierkegaard was likely a very brilliant man. I believe this brilliance, in conjunction with a largely ignorant and shortsighted society, drove him to be increasingly frustrated and bewildered, eventually causing him to depart from the wisdom of the Word due to a lack of spiritual guidance (and meaningful fellowship) in practice (a common problem for many people). As a result, he found it increasingly difficult to effectively communicate and this directly influenced his methods of communication. I have some pity for him due to this struggle. I would imagine that, if given the proper learning environment and life guidance, he would have proven a valuable contributor not to the increasingly depraved humanity that chooses to deify him, but instead a great contributor to the cause of Christ.

Our popular culture today grasps its firm hold on existentialism, wielding it as a tool to further the hedonistic desires of mankind (and, ultimately, Satan) while communicating the justification for their increasing selfishness. And, as the next catchy vocal verse or addictive melody is released to the thrill of mankind, it is almost impossible to not find direct existentialist principles in those songs, regardless of the genre of music. Just compare the top 40 hit lyrics of today with the music sang 200 years ago. Satan has successfully tethered the power of existentialism to effectively indoctrinate people to eventually demand that others not judge them. Sometimes they even invoke the words of Christ (or the word "god") to prove their point (or provide their justification), without considering the immediate Biblical context not to mention the message of the whole Word.

As it stands, Kierkegaard used common human experience and self-repressed emotions to cloud his brilliance and directly influence a system of flawed logic that eventually demands the amplification of the human experience and causes the overwhelming doubt of a will of God and purpose for living the Christian life. It may not have been exactly what Kierkegaard wanted to convey or genuinely communicate to mankind, but it was exactly what a depraved humanity wanted to discover, embrace and further the development of.

"For the wisdom of this world is foolishness with God. For it is written, "He catches the wise in their own craftiness"; and again, "The LORD knows the thoughts of the wise, that they are futile." Therefore let no one boast in men. For all things are yours: whether Paul or Apollos or Cephas, or the world or life or death, or things present or things to come--all are yours. And you are Christ's, and Christ is God's." 1 Corinthians 3:19-23, NKJV.

CHAPTER 12

Mr. Breese closes *Seven Men* with a final, 12th, chapter. We will eventually go on forward to the 13th chapter in this book to cover the one subject that Breese was simply unable to address at the time of writing and publishing his book. For now, back to chapter 12.

Every earnest reader and learner will be forced to admit that *Seven Men* will have certainly left its mark indelibly on their mind. Most readers who are moved and impressed by the book will likely yearn for a copy in their personal library. Undoubtedly, the logical progressions and information provided in the simple (yet reasonably comprehensive) book that Breese provided to mankind will linger and be built upon by the submissive child of God as they communicate to family, friends and neighbors regarding humanism and the problems of their modern society.

The final chapter of *Seven Men* provides final thoughts and instructions for action by Mr. Breese. Again, in light of the now historical period of the last 25 years (a quarter century!) since the first publishing of this volume (and, obviously, the just as old or even older authorship by Mr. Breese), it is both interesting and chilling to read his closing thoughts as put down in this extremely influential book.

Ultimately, this final chapter focuses directly on the beseeching of Pastor Breese concerning the then solely future actions of Bible believing and respecting individuals. No doubt Mr. Breese may have felt hope and capability to influence culture and individual minds for the cause of Christ was rapidly slipping from between the figurative fingers of our Christian society (even in those days). He uses this chapter to try to provide a voice to the reversal of such a tenuous grasp on the modern American culture.

Sadly, in light of recent history (and, if past results are any indication of future performance), it does appear that the entreating nature of his guidance appears to have been largely in vain (as will be mine). Not only were his words never adopted widespread across Christianity, they (and his overall legacy) have faded largely into obscurity. This is not indicative of the lack of quality of his message or means of providing said message, it is more indicative of, as

Breese might have said himself, his words were NOT what humanity was searching for at the time.

And that is truly the overall arc of the book. If this reader was forced to choose a concept to summarize the material found in this book, it would be that, regardless of the men characterized and covered in this volume, it is really the widespread demanded adoption of the teachings and philosophies of these men by society to place them squarely into the position of being seven of the men who rule from the grave.

The term "adoption" as I wrote in the preceding paragraph above is only a portion of the full meaning I am attempting to convey which will be fulfilled society wide in a soon to be seen future time. The full meaning of the concept goes beyond learning, adoption and unquestioned implementation (read: indoctrination). It goes to the full depth, breadth and width of worship. That worship is not solely of the seven men outlined in this volume, it is the complete and total worship of humanity as a whole. Mankind is not capable of serving two masters, as outlined in the Word of God (Matthew 6:24 amongst other references), so they easily throw aside the truth of the Word so that they can do their level best to personally attain the sovereign power of the true Creator God for themselves (a pursuit that human society has embraced, ebbing and flowing, throughout the sands of time). And, it is with that apparent conflict and eventuality that Breese frames the organization and instruction in this book.

We began with the insidious teachings of the "Devil's Clergyman", Charles Darwin. His concepts (which were not truly and wholly of his own sole originality as many of "his" concepts were taught two millennium prior (!) but were conveyed by himself in a manner undeniably effective) first caused the widespread doubt of the validity of the Bible and its account of history. In its place we see the theory of evolution being provided as the sole socially acceptable method of viewing and interpreting history. This method of viewing and interpreting history (natural and otherwise) has a set of principles and philosophies that are now being fully brought to bear on the engineering of the future. For, if humanity does not serve God and is largely the result of a series of chemical/life cycle accidents, then humanity is truly the universe's underdog. And, now that the tide has turned in favor of the power of humanity, it is time to use that power and capability to assure our permanent place in the universe. It is now time to engineer the perfect, utopian future.

Man, who was once something far less than even an earthworm in function and capability in the view of evolutionary scientists, must now prohibit anything less than our ideal desires as a society. The theory of evolution taught as genuine and unequivocal history must eventually evolve itself into a view of controlling humanity and propelling a greater agenda of society as determined by those who are the strongest or "fittest". We are now on the cusp of such a train of thought and its overwhelming ramifications for an increasingly depraved mankind.

Consider this: all of this mind-altering philosophy put into place by one book authored by one man less than 200 years ago (though in truth the thought process and philosophy is as old as the Ionian coast of Greece and her philosophers). It was not the fact that Darwin was correct in his assumptions or far exceeding the intellectual power of all other humans, a man of omniscience, a beacon of truth shining into the dark ages to revive the hope of humanity. It is not truly the actions of Darwin that convinced the populace. No, instead, it was just enough foolishness to distract some, amplify others and enable all of a depraved and rebellious humanity to believe whatever it was they wanted to believe. It was that Darwin's literary release enabled an unbelieving humanity to move forward as they had had always wanted to act. It gave mankind the beginnings of a cohesive strategy and the first widely visible germinations of the seed that was planted in the garden thousands of years prior by Satan himself when he tempted Eve.

And, when we (as humanity in toto) question the meaning and validity of the Word of God, when we challenge the attributes of the Sovereign Creator God, when we rebel against His program for morality and His system of natural law, when we dispute His power and beauty of creation, we invite all manner of evil into the realm of our existence. Darwin unlocked the gate and hell (or the principles and increasing capabilities thereof) burst through. Yet, a depraved humanity claims he brought about enlightenment, that he has empowered wisdom for all.

Once craftily questioned, once openly denied, once disrespected without concern, the truth becomes very hard to adhere to, especially when adhering to the truth is the most difficult pathway to functioning in the human experience. Therefore, since humans are inherently rebellious against God and truly disinterested in honest effort with humble returns (in any realm of human reality), the truth becomes irrelevant. In its place is an engineered set of policies or procedures and a program the embraces the weaknesses of humanity as its greatest strengths. We go from an environment of complete truth to increasing fabrication; culminating in what is for all intents and purposes, a world without accurate truth or God respecting morality.

The trend of fabricated truths and evil philosophies began to increase immediately thereafter the publication of Darwin's contribution to the depravity of the world. From Marx (and his cadre), who applied the evolutionary principles not to science and the origin of mankind but instead directly to society and government, to Wellhausen, who brought the evolutionary principle - via the philosophy of spiritual evolution - straight to the pulpits and pews of religious groups across the face of the earth. From the reality questioning doctrines of Freud to the ideal method of distribution of the message/indoctrination as devised by John Dewey. From the economic logistical support of Keynes to the subtle means of exploiting the every day common experience of mankind as was begun to be developed by Kierkegaard; there is no doubt that these seven men have made their own diabolical legacy on the hearts and minds of all men. For some of these men, their goal was open rebellion against God and His program. For others, it may have been less evil. However, all of them play an important role in the manipulation of humanity to meet the will of Satan (the great puppeteer himself). But, as mentioned before, these seven men were not - by themselves – solely responsible for the depravity that has followed them. They but planted the seed that mankind was all too eager to foster, protect and harvest for self-profit. They provided that which mankind increasingly wanted and demanded to hear.

Breese does not entitle the volume "The *Seven Men*", perhaps indicating that either he believed that there were potentially more than the seven he outlines, or that he left room for others yet to come. As Breese had some significant background in eschatology, it would not surprise me if he had intended us to assume that there might be others yet to come. Who knows if, one day many years from now, another book is published along the same lines, criteria and thought process entitled "Eleven Men" outlining four others to add to the list Breese already assembled.

John Dewey provided the means by which the indoctrination of humanity could begin at the most tender and young ages of each individual. And, we can see that this indoctrination completely alters the mindset of a person if given the opportunity to do so. If allowed to take root and grow, it becomes increasingly difficult to eradicate it from the mind of those exposed to the process of indoctrination. However, it is possible to "deprogram" a person who has been systematically manipulated. The means to discovering God given reality must first come from the desire of a person to seek said truth (however that first is manifested in their life). It requires the complete humility of a person before God to begin the process of correcting their flawed and rebellious thought process. The rescue from the lying and controlling methods of the world, which culminates with the individual eternal suffering and damnation of all unbelievers can only come through the regeneration and reconciliation made possible by Jesus Christ. Without that spiritual change, no man has any genuine hope.

So pervasive and complete is the satanic program that no person alive today can escape being directly influenced in some way by it. And, only by faithfully learning the Word of God, ministry to others and humility before God can a person ever hope to be on a pathway towards recovery from the vacuum of Satan that will utterly destroy every God-denying man, woman or child. There is a means of escape from the destruction that will come. You can overcome the impending destruction of humanity and our current social example of the world. You can exchange the fallacy for truth and eternal reward.

The last chapter is entitled "Who Shall Overcome" and it is here that we see the basic tenants of rescue, the identification of those who have the hope of overcoming this horrible conspiracy against God and universal justice. We see in chapter 12 of *Seven Men* a two-fold look at the realms from which we can find rescue. First, Breese surely identifies a means for temporal rescue from the physical world around us by an immediate altering of our social habits to more closely relate to Biblical morals. He stresses (and I would contend he does so correctly) that the God-honoring alteration of social habits had to have been accomplished in a very quick, sudden and complete motion in order to have any earthly hope in the potential culture-wide correction of church age (and largely God neglecting) humanity. This was, in light of history, not to be produced in short order and now 25 years has passed. My position is that it is completely beyond the realm of reality to imagine it is more possible now than it was then. In fact, I am quite pessimistic in regard to any earthly hope for a long-term God fearing prognosis. I believe that we missed the boat on this one (for various reasons, not the least of which was a failure of the Christian church as a body) and mankind will never again come to widespread humility before God during this age we now reside within.

With daily atrocities such as the placement of hundreds of wire coat hangers inserted into the ground in coordinated college campus events, the prospect and practice of burning aborted human babies for grid electricity (as medical "waste") and polyamorous homosexual marriage being highlighted by the media as "the new normal", it does appear quite possible that the creation of God is in full and open rebellion against Him. Their rebellion is obviously self-destructive, but they have simply convinced themselves that it makes the most sense to be so inclined. For them, life has little meaning and they use this philosophy/worldview to influence their every life choice.

The second type of rescue that Breese identifies directly regards the eternal future which will, for those of us who believe in Christ alone, be a transition from physical to spiritual to the ultimate manifestation as the "whole man" (both physical perfection and spiritual completeness). It is this hope that is still very much available to all of mankind who wishes for said hope. The simplest means of identifying those who shall eternally overcome the program of Satan and its beyond imagination torture and suffering is perhaps this:

Those who have accepted the natural fact that Christ is the Son of God and rely solely upon His actions as a means of reconciling themselves to God. Christ, the perfect once for all sacrifice who made us co-crucified, co-buried, co-risen and co-heirs, providing our spiritual position in Him for rescue by God.

We who recognize Jesus Christ as messiah shall eternally overcome. It may be painful in the short term as we see our Heavenly Father and all that which is right and perfectly placed by God suffer at the hands of a depraved humanity and its leader, Satan. But Dave Breese surely placed the basic foundation into place to begin to have a greater understanding of the state of the world, why it is in that state, how to escape the demonized lies of Satan and how to take some solace and temporary relief in the truth as provided by God in His Word. We can use this information to edify ourselves, minister unto others, and remain vigilant and rejoice in the eternal hope we who have answered His call now have.

Seven Men is a valuable treatise for every intelligent and considering person alive today. It has the power and capability to completely change their worldview to closer ally itself with the truth as provided by God in our blessed gift, the Word of God, our Holy Bible. But, to simply read *Seven Men* and to place it on the shelf to gather dust is an injustice to Dr. Dave Breese, to your neighbors, family, friends, co-workers, and to yourself. Introduce the information presented to you in your thought process in conjunction to an increasing maturity in Gods Word and put it into daily practice. Demonstrate this wisdom and demand the same from those that you can influence.

None of us are made perfect in these "broken vessels" and we will all fail from time to time, but what is your normal stance towards God? Do you spend time in His Word and in fellowship with other believers walking along the same lines? Do you aim to improve for the cause of Christ? How do you display that to others? This is the best way to assist a society increasingly depraved and spiritually adrift. This is the only true warfare we can wage against Satan in this day and age. This is the best way that we can effectively serve our Heavenly Father.

CHAPTER 13

Oh, what a difference a few years can make.

Seven Men was published in 1990, prior to the explosion of interconnected (networked) computer technology, supercomputing, artificial intelligence and robotics. There was no reasonable expectation that Dave Breese could have fully envisioned the rapidity or means of the recent advent of evil that has interconnected the various strains of diabolical philosophy and indoctrination covered both in *Seven Men* as well as this volume. The flourishing of the silicon-based technologies surrounding and enveloping us today have forever transformed the previously widely disconnected individual dogmatic components into a type of mass delusion that stretches its influence across all segments of our population today. Technology itself is not truly to blame for the pseudo-truths and social dysfunction permeating the fabric of our collective landscape. Instead, technology reflects the focus, pursuit, relative genius, failings and most intimate desires of mankind. And those intimate desires - when paralleling with the desires and plan of Satan – lead mankind into distraction, eternally ineffectual efforts, relatively empty lives and into opposition to God Himself.

In 1990, the internet (as first experienced by the hoi polloi) was still being designed and generally expected common standards had not yet come to fruition. It is obvious that, for essentially everyone in society at the time of the release of *Seven Men*, very few had ever even considered such a thought as the now everyday and every where internet all people have become accustomed to and, frankly, dependent upon. In the space of a quarter of a century our world went from being independent and unaware of silicon-based technology and the internet to being addicted and wholly dependent upon it. Like an abused drug, the internet has stolen many things from the intrinsic meaning of mankind and yet somehow makes the abuser oddly shameless and oblivious to their increasing moral bankruptcy.

By 1993 there were but a scant 50 HTTP servers available. HTTP servers are the type of internet linked computer that people use with their web browser (also known simply as a "browser"). At the end of

1995 there were over 16 million internet users. In 2000 there were 304 million and in December of 2005 there were over one billion users. Today, upon publication of this volume, there are over 3 billion active and unique users of the internet on all seven continents of the globe. In the span of less than 20 years essentially half of the entire world population became active regular users of the internet. And, current estimates widely circulate claiming that over 5 billion people will be active regular users of the internet by 2020. This will be the vast majority of the global population.

For many individuals, and perhaps most people, this growth will signal prosperity, progress and amazing human achievement. No doubt, it will be assumed to be a segue to usher in a new era of peace, collaboration and equality for all mankind. The internet will be found virtually everywhere, given enough time. Research and development regarding global internet coverage is active and ongoing even as this book is compiled.

Breese passed into glory in 2002. To our detriment, he did not revise his book with the inclusion of pervasive computing, the internet and its effects upon society. Perhaps he felt that it was not necessary (perhaps he did not recognize the implications of the adoption of this social platform throughout the masses), futile to discuss the subject, or he could not secure the funding and expertise to make a quality revision.

However, his lack of revision does not diminish the current necessity to include a chapter here regarding the role that social media and broadband (high-speed) internet, along with an "always-on" and "interconnected" mentality (all made possible through silicon-based technology) has played in the rising tide of unified humanism throughout contemporary society.

My first experience with the internet came in early 1992 and the experience was best described as the computerized version of traveling across the wild west frontiers of the Oregon Trail of the 1850's (the so-called "internet" or "information superhighway" as seen from a modern consumer standpoint experience is nothing like the internet people encountered back in those "pioneering" days). My teenage eyes lit up like neon lights as I saw the enormous potential for the technology. My father appeared non-committal, and perhaps even hesitant, although he was a savvy computer user himself.

As internet technology became more simple, reliable and relevant to daily life, so too did the number of internet users increase as seen above. What was once never heard of or imagined in the mind of men is now widely discussed as the most important development in the history of the world, rivaling or perhaps even exceeding nuclear technologies.

Nuclear power and weaponry requires massive amounts of research, capital and logistics. To be facetious or to authentically describe an individual who is incredibly intelligent a person may use the metaphor, "Well, look who's the nuclear scientist!" Nuclear science and the development of nuclear energy or weapons is complicated, intellectually intense and globally regulated/monitored.

The standard home user does not have access to uranium, plutonium, or any other significantly radioactive material in amounts or quality necessary to generate their own electricity. Even owning the equipment required to search for these objects proves to be expensive and difficult to obtain. You don't see suburban neighbors renting backhoes and digging holes in their yard while mining for uranium deposits for them to enrich into fission reactor quality fuel for their home. In fact, radioactive material is so hazardous and alarming to the general public that many become nervous in the mere presence of a radioactivity warning sign.

The "Cold War" of the post World War II era horrified humanity and sent social shock waves across the United States as people considered, for the first time, massive physical destruction raining down upon them from half a world away. In the time it would take for the turn of a key, the press of a button and the flight of a rocket (and there were thousands of those rockets), their lives would be forever changed or perhaps even ended. Within minutes the fires and destruction that we once only imagined in the realm of Satan and his hell became tangible reality at the whim of our foes.

Bomb shelters became all the rage as husbands, fathers, wives and mothers all searched for ways to protect their families and themselves from the almost inevitable onslaught of unimaginable ruination. Catalogs, door to door salesman and ex-car dealers now turned "underground architectural engineers" all promised the security and "peace of mind" of these bomb shelters. Of course, some shelters were superior to others and even a few installed shelters would have provided some realistic protection from the initial blast wave and radioactive fallout to follow the attack that society knew was only a matter of time to come upon them. But, sadly, many shelters offered little or no genuine protection.

Local, state and federal governments spent countless millions to provide audio and video instruction in the case of these attacks. One government opportunity entitled the National Fallout Shelter Program encouraged the building, stocking and registration of fallout shelters across the United States. The general public felt that it was their duty to know where these fallout shelters were and prepare themselves for the eventuality of escaping into one of these facilities. It was a serious, lifesaving business that might just keep themselves and their children alive.

Yet, today, in spite of all of the obvious warning signs and examples of personal danger, something more dangerous than nuclear war or a meltdown at a nuclear power reactor is paraded as the beautiful crown jewel of the next level of human social justice and glory. It is the internet. And, no matter what might transpire, there appears to be no way to educate the public about its dangers, both real in the here and now and those dangers yet to come. Perhaps because the danger is not in the technology itself but is actually within almost every person, intrinsically tied to their soul and willingness to abuse their relationship with God.

The public has embraced the internet and appear to be incapable of ever letting go of their fixation. There is rarely a home found that does not have multiple internet connected devices operating within its walls. What was once a computer isolated on the entire floor of a skyscraper, then found on the desks and living rooms of every school and home in the civilized world is now carried in a pocket, bag, purse or on the bridge of nose or a wrist. And, one day, that technology will be tied even more physically to each individual.

Government entities are increasingly mandating the use of interconnected internet based technologies amongst their citizens, every business has a website and almost every individual citizen has a social media account as well as an increasing desire to consume more internet based content all of the time.

The internet (in its many forms) is perhaps the greatest common distraction (or, facilitator of distraction) from God as licensed and empowered by its users. Amongst so many other things propelled by Satan (literally, anything not focused upon God and living a Godly life as stipulated by His Holy Word), it is used to keep people distracted and occupied in pursuits that encourage the abuse of our relationship with the truly Sovereign Creator God and our healthy respect and consideration for each other. Those technology supported pursuits take various forms, not all of which may be found solely or mainly "online".

The internet, as viewed by God, is irrelevant to His creation. It is but foolishness to Him as it is unnecessary and unbeneficial in His perfect environment and eternal plan/program. The internet, in eternity future, will cease to exist and will pass into intellectual oblivion.

Particularly distressing is the amount of distraction the internet poses for those who believe in God and are reconciled to Him through Jesus Christ. A belief in Christ does not immunize a willing mind and spirit against the distractions of Satan any more than belief will suddenly resolve all sin nature tendencies within the reconciled believer. And, for those who hold a higher level of duty toward dedicating their lives to Him and His Word in their lives (as they are to be increasingly effective ambassadors of Christ), the internet can quickly lead His servants away from their duty.

Also highly concerning is the ability for the internet to make things change or disappear, so-to-speak. Once important and valuable works and information can be deleted or blocked with a very little time and effort. Censoring of Biblical information may be the order of the day in the very near future. The determination about what content an end user can experience is decided without warning and without review. Just the mere possibility of altering a tiny fraction of the Word (or Biblically based information) could alter the entire meaning of the original point conveyed by the author of the information. If a video or article online meets enough resistance, its validity is not considered by those outside of the firestorm the original content may have created. Instead, Biblically valuable content can be disabled or traffic will be rerouted and the individuals doing this will be the enemies of the Bible.

Some people would contend that I am overstating the danger here; that I am perhaps even overreacting. And, before I give the wrong impression, let me reiterate my position. The internet itself is not the problem, per se, and can be used in edifying ways. The internet is a tool, a tool no different than a shovel, a dishwasher, a rifle or an eggbeater. As with those other tools, there are effective uses for the internet and irresponsible methods of use as well.

The internet is necessarily amoral (as is everything not directly and originally created by God). It is something that is inanimate and incapable of naturally recognizing morality. It has no soul, no intrinsic character, no volition and no self-identity. It does not deserve a please nor a thank you. It does not get its feelings hurt, linger in love or necessarily endure insecurity or fear. It is not natural, nor part of God's initial, unrefined creation. It will never be anything more than artificial and programmed (even if that programming is self-programmed via "artificial intelligence"). Eventually, God will destroy it as well as the intrinsic sin nature and foolish desires in the heart of all in His eternal presence.

The real problem is not with the artificially created and programmed internet. The genuine problem is the way people, in general, react to the internet. Just as the stones used to build the tower of Babel were not to blame for the design and will of the builders, so the wires, switches, computers, radios and fiber optics of the internet cannot bear the blame for the anti-God sentiments and humanist agenda that mankind is using via the internet (amongst other means) to accelerate and globally propagate their plan (either actively or passively) of opposition to God. *The problem is not genuinely technology, it is the communication level that mankind is capable of attaining/establishing via that technology.* Satan exploits the weaknesses of mankind at every turn and communication coupled with technology is the devil's favorite play toy (quite literally).

How does this fit in with the *Seven Men* and the larger diabolical conspiracy to distract and manipulate humanity? It's really quite simple:

Most of the seven men included in the Breese book existed in a time in which communication technology was poorly developed and regional at best. People, until well into the British Colonial period of world history, primarily lived within and rarely ventured outside of a few square miles of their home. In order for Marx to communicate with people in California, for example, he would have had to have had months of waiting for even only two letters to exchange. If he wanted to visit his California recipient in person, it was a huge and somewhat dangerous undertaking, not to mention the expense of such a trip. Even if he arrived safely, it took weeks and sometimes longer to make the trip in person, dependent upon the age of travel we would be observing. Today, the collected works of Marx can be transmitted freely over the internet in a matter of minutes or perhaps even seconds. Books (or even a short passage of a particular book) that were once very difficult to come by can, today, be found readily in various formats for all devices in all countries.

If Marx existed today (2014) he could choose to simply share his daily diatribes in short snippets of 150 characters or fewer to his increasing millions of followers. He might share his hourly status with his friends, families, collaborators and students. Karl might have even decided to make a series of videos that he would offer for free on a website visited by hundreds of millions of people daily. Whatever might "get the message out" and continue the "education" of his subscribers. Boy, how Karl Marx missed out on that indoctrinating "gravy train"!

Or did he? Karl Marx lives on in our current internet crazed inter-connected society. So does Darwin, Wellhausen, Freud, Dewey, all of them. Even Thales, Plato, Socrates, all of whom existed thousands of years ago, are still readily accessible after a few taps on the touchscreen. It is not the internet technology that enables their message to spread and anchor itself amongst the mentalities of the masses, it is the increasing depravity of humanity as briefly explained by Mr. Breese on page 68 (amongst other locations) of *Seven Men*.

Nicholas Carr has written a book entitled *The Shallows* that does a solid and credible job of illustrating the effect that the internet has had (and continues to have) on the human mind (albeit from a secular standpoint). Tangible physical changes are increasingly observable as are the effects seen in our society today. Shorter attention spans, trouble with establishing and maintaining concentration, lack of effective memory storage, obsessive behavior are all common and perhaps expected in our modern internet enabled device centered societies.

There are seriously debilitating repercussions for the common internet connected device user accustomed to being bombarded with content on an increasing basis. They have allowed themselves to enter a world of distraction. And those distractions do not, contrary to public opinion, increase mental faculty by any means. While many people consider themselves superior to generations prior due to their ability to more easily relate to and function with electronic gadgets, "multitask" better and have – at least this can be said true for the most adept at using these devices – become information brokers, they are simply more amenable to their programming as researched and developed by Satan himself and willingly implemented by mankind.

Unfortunately, these distractions and newly valued capabilities, so praised and acclaimed by society, actually cause people to spend less time contemplating that which they are bombarded by. They are increasingly incapable of critical cognitive skills and necessary decision-making based upon genuine factors involved in the situation. Instead, they are simply more skillfully programmed to respond as pre-determined by others. Seen individually, this truth is disturbing. On a socially wide scale it is completely catastrophic.

Simply put, societies are made up of collections of individuals. Therefore, the distractions influencing more and more individuals will eventually be first disastrous and finally fatal to society and humanity, as we have known them.

C.S. Lewis wrote a very intriguing treatise on the subject of humanity surrendering themselves willingly to technology (particularly the purported "educated", the politicians, the community organizing segments of society (or, *change agents* as coined by Charlotte Thomson Iserbyt)) entitled *The Abolition of Man*. His premise is that most of mankind is supremely accommodating to the thought of the increase of technology for all of its obvious benefits. However, a select few choose what these benefits are at any given time, how they are developed, how they are distributed, and what the purpose is of those temporary beneficial values. All of this is done on high (so-to-speak) with an eye towards "improving" individual humanity and society as a whole. Unfortunately, this equates to a very small segment of the populace deciding what is best for the whole. And, the whole is led into this controlled position via the "benefits" of technology. Although C.S. Lewis did not distinctly mention the mentally distracting power of technology in *Abolition*, it is nonetheless a very true and debilitating circumstance, demonstrated daily by billions.

Beneath (or behind) all of that which we have discussed thus far is the diabolical plan of world domination that will literally enslave mankind to the wishes and whim of their cruel and unjust master, Satan. Defeat (death and eternal separation from God) is being snatched from the jaws of victory (as provided for all humanity throughout the ages by the actions of the Lord Jesus Christ, once for all who genuinely accept it) and the master (of the individual mind) is becoming the enslaved (to the collective), just as he (Satan) has planned. But, as with so many examples through the annals of history, mankind will not readily swerve away from their diabolical destination. The *Seven Men* portrayed and discussed in Breese's volume had individual portions of the blueprint for this world domination. The internet has allowed the amalgamation and implementation of the final product as demanded by a willing and short-sighted global society.

There are two other concerning components of our current globalized society that need to be addressed prior to the end of this chapter. The first involves the need for increasing mental stimulus through entertainment and the second is the addictive mentality that many individuals possess today.

Many people are increasingly incapable of applying themselves to any tasks not related directly to the device they hold and the internet that device accesses. People have become quite comfortable exchanging reality for the virtual (artificial) environment they can find online. So much so that they are readily and voluntarily exchanging tangible reality for the virtual online environment that they psychologically establish as "genuine". This is becoming true of almost all demographic segments of society, regardless of continent. Technology is lauded as such an aid to humanity, and in fact can be very useful and labor relieving. However, something the Word clearly illustrates to us (repeatedly and throughout) is the inability of mankind to know their limitations, boundaries and reasonable actions. We call these obvious failures "being human" and they are touted as intrinsic to life as is breathing oxygen.

In our society demanding first democracy, and eventually socialism and communism, you can expect that "being human" will be amplified right along with all of the supposed benefits of humanism. The difference is that "being human" will be celebrated and no longer considered detrimental in any sense (there will be no objective Godly morality to base "right" and "wrong" off of - given time). And with that celebration of humanity will come no widespread recognition of sin or the sinful nature of each individual. Instead, the consciousness of sin will simply fade away as Satan and his dominion take an ever-increasing grasp on society. All of this will be a distraction from the supernatural reality of the situation.

The *Seven Men* in the book by Mr. Breese created the pathway for mankind to meet the goals of Satan and the technology of the internet has facilitated the plan and message of those seven individuals to become relevant and cohesive in ways never before possible. In fact, the internet allows a sinful, disobedient and God disrespecting humanity to exploit technology for the purpose of fostering and harvesting the ideals and philosophies of the seven men (and, ultimately, Satan) while encouraging those ideals to swell and exponentially reproduce their invasive growth in the hearts and minds of an increasing number of individuals.

The new social tendencies of the people increasingly tethered to technology and the "interconnected" and "collaborative" circles that develop around these device/connected users allow for those inside said circles to be more easily programmed (or reprogrammed) by the loudest voices, the most influential special interest groups and/or the most intellectually and emotionally pleasing forces. Their short attention span and even shorter memory life directly impact their logical thought process while their craving for increasing stimulus causes them to be less tolerant of challenges and difficulties in their personal lives while they pursue new and greater stimuli. In turn, they demand less challenge, less difficulty and they become more willing to endure losing some rights and responsibilities to ensure their stimulus and a temporary (or even false) limiting or alleviation of challenge and difficulty.

Eventually, these reprogrammed people generally begin to categorize only the result of events in one of two groups of emotional response: "good" (or "pleasing") or "bad" (or "displeasing") and they forget or discard the vital components of cause that created those events. In a way, they become so fixated on their personal gain (and avoiding personal loss or displeasure) that they mindlessly surrender certain things they do not effectively utilize as they assume they will not ever miss their presence in their life. And, those doing the programming/reprogramming have found the best means of making those concessions appear negligible or of no consequence whatsoever.

This is the goal of Satan. Humanity - as a whole - is playing entirely into his game, into his program. Satan yearns to control and eventually enslave or destroy the glorious creation of God called humanity. The reasons why are simple; humanity is made in God's image (Genesis 1:27) and Satan desires to usurp God so he may ascend to the controller of all in existence, both heaven and earth (Is. 14:13-14). We are the only part of God's creation that is made entirely in His image. Since Satan considers God to be his arch nemesis, why wouldn't Satan first attempt to enslave man and then destroy them (or, perhaps more accurately, allow them to destroy themselves)? Satan is well aware that he does not yet have the capability to overthrow God (nor will he ever have this power, only his deluded and entirely depraved mind can allow him to believe that he will ever have that capability) so in the meantime he will instead manipulate, distract and deceive those who are most like God, humanity.

And, as illustrated those thousands of years ago in the Garden of Eden, mankind is ultimately willing to allow this to occur, as they intrinsically believe that they will have the upper hand over Satan (as well as God), that they can outlast, outwit and outplay Satan (and God) himself.

To reiterate, the problem is truly not the internet or technology itself. In fact, there are many, many examples of reasonable and good use for the internet (some of which I personally employ). God proves even now to use a plan of Satan for the good of individuals who humble themselves before Him and recognize the truth of His Word by grace alone through faith alone.

Instead, it is the exploitive nature and situational ethics of Satan and humanity that are really the issue that allows humanity to function as it is now and will wax criminally while most members of society believe that they are committing increasingly righteous acts for the good of all mankind.

The root of the problem is generations old, and is typical of a God-challenging humanity with a volition (free will) who opposes the perfect plan of God, at times without ever really knowing why. The problem is that mankind does not want to submit to the wishes and morality of their Creator. Instead, just as Satan so dearly (in fact, *desperately*) desires, they wish to flex their proverbial muscle and have *THEIR* will be done. And, some people will be willing to do whatever it takes to see that desire made manifest.

The seven men in the book as authored by Mr. Breese all wished for their will to be done (likely with direct demonic influence) and the modern technologies (as well as those yet to come) are the conduit that has created the confluence of their plans to first be fleshed out and then implemented increasingly wholesale.

God can - and will - stop the madness at His pleasure and in His good time. And, it is a blessing for humanity that he continues to be longsuffering; (II Peter 3) as it is solely via this character of His that an increasingly depraved humanity even has an opportunity to come into reconciliation with Him. For those who do not believe, time is growing shorter by the second, submit to Him and accept the gift of grace through faith in the Lord Jesus Christ! Consider what God provided to you through the Word, specifically for the purpose of reconciling Himself to you.

If you already believe in God through the Lord Jesus Christ alone, spread this message of longsuffering to all of mankind before God advances His program and increase in the joy of your eternal Heavenly citizenship. Either way, prepare yourself for the occurrence of the diabolical orchestration of the failure of human society worldwide.

Appendix I

I am including these examples of the widespread socially accepted (perhaps even expected and sanctioned?) rebellion of humanity against the One True Creator God so that the reader may analyze the diabolical program of Satan as expressed by his willing disciples (straight from the horses mouth, so-to-speak). As you read through these, consider what portions are open insults to the truth of His Word and towards our loving God Himself. Also consider how these tenants influence society as a whole through entertainment, "news", education, inter-personal relationships, etc. Notice how subtle some of the deceptions are and how some of the tenants mirror or parallel the truths of the Word and God's superior morality.

As you analyze each word, recognize the lack of submission to God and the amplification of human solutions to the problems that plague mankind. Until mankind submits wholly and genuinely before God and respects His plan and program for life as identified and communicated in the Word of God (The Holy Bible), there will be no genuine resolution or lasting peace for humanity. Bear in mind that their every word undermines the Bible and is disrespectful of the Sovereign God of the entire universe (either actively or passively).

"Adulterers and adulteresses! Do you not know that friendship with the world is enmity with God? Whoever therefore wants to be a friend of the world makes himself an enemy of God." James 4:4, NKJV.

The following appendix is, to a degree, annotated. Annotated comments by this author are provided solely in **boldface** and *italicized* type placed directly below the section in discussion.

Humanist Manifesto I (1933)

The Manifesto is a product of many minds. It was designed to represent a developing point of view, not a new creed. The individuals whose signatures appear would, had they been writing individual statements, have stated the propositions in differing terms. The importance of the document is that more than thirty men have come to general agreement on matters of final concern and that these men are undoubtedly representative of a large number who are forging a new philosophy out of the materials of the modern world. -- Raymond B. Bragg (1933)

Forging a new philosophy that is in open rebellion against God and His morality. Sadly, the failure of the Christian church as a whole allowed this effort to find some initial validity in the minds of the populace.

The time has come for widespread recognition of the radical changes in religious beliefs throughout the modern world. The time is past for mere revision of traditional attitudes. Science and economic change have disrupted the old beliefs. Religions the world over are under the necessity of coming to terms with new conditions created by a vastly increased knowledge and experience. In every field of human activity, the vital movement is now in the direction of a candid and explicit humanism. In order that religious humanism may be better understood we, the undersigned, desire to make certain affirmations which we believe the facts of our contemporary life demonstrate.

This author could not agree more wholeheartedly with the necessity to recognize the radical differences in religious beliefs throughout the modern world (as all approaches save for an explicit faith in the Lord Jesus Christ is spiritual foolishness and open rebellion against the Father and His sovereignty and plan). And, in truth, traditional attitudes (or even church teachings) were not always (nor are they currently) indicative of the truth of the Word of God. It is this divergence of the stance of the organized Christian church and the Word of God - literally interpreted and in common practice - that has failed to meet the needs of society. The Holy Spirit has been given to true believers that they might bring the light of God's wisdom, grace and action to the world in varying degrees. As the organized church has chosen, in most historic examples, to compromise and surrender socioeconomic/moral ground to the fallacies of humanism.

There is great danger of a final, and we believe fatal, identification of the word religion with doctrines and methods which have lost their significance and which are powerless to solve the problem of human living in the Twentieth Century. Religions have

80

always been means for realizing the highest values of life. Their end has been accomplished through the interpretation of the total environing situation (theology or world view), the sense of values resulting therefrom (goal or ideal), and the technique (cult), established for realizing the satisfactory life. A change in any of these factors results in alteration of the outward forms of religion. This fact explains the changefulness of religions through the centuries. But through all changes religion itself remains constant in its quest for abiding values, an inseparable feature of human life.

A quick note here on the difference between that which is "religious" and that which is truly "spiritual". The change brought about by faith in the Lord Jesus Christ, being a recipient of a new birth (John 3:3) and permanently indwelt by the Holy Spirit, is an internal and very personal change. This change is intrinsically connected to the believer and is everlasting, for all of eternity. Those benefits have been presented and prepared for each individual believer so that they may provide edification and assistance to their fellow man and service to the Lord. As a corporate group, Christians are only as healthy as their leadership and individual submission to God Himself. This includes every Christian meeting in any type of facility, from the largest cathedral to the smallest home assembly. No specific church is endowed or empowered with special gifts from God that did not first come to the individual at the very first moment of their belief. From the time of belief a Christian is provided with their spiritual empowerment. It is then only the replacement of human philosophies via Biblical truths in action (also known as that which is truly called "ministry") that must be accomplished by an individual.

The world that is not living in grace through faith in the Lord Jesus Christ considers all "Christian churches" to be cut of the same, or at least very similar, cloth (and they call this cloth "religion"). In truth, the denomination of the Christian church or particular group reflects only one basic truth: many individuals who claim Christ as their Savior are not constantly willing and vigilant to do the effort and submission necessary to place the Word of God - literally interpreted - at the center of their daily life. This transformation is a process. As it is a process, it is something that those dedicated to that process will successfully transcend in starts and fits throughout their life. For those who ignore or reject the process, they will lie spiritually stagnant in their state of belief. And, it is this simple root cause that is primarily responsible for the numerous and increasing examples of failures of Christian churches both close to home and global in reach.

Religion is widely defined by the populace as any practice of supernatural worship. That is, the worship of anything that is greater than an individual can alone attain. For humanists, this religion is the human collective. For Muslims, this is Allah and their recognized prophet. For cosmotheists, this is a greater life energy of the cosmos.

So, as you can see, the two terms are not truly synonyms, no matter what an unbeliever might propose.

Also consider the new religion that humanists have established, the worship of mankind and their accomplishments.

Today man's larger understanding of the universe, his scientific achievements, and deeper appreciation of brotherhood, have created a situation which requires a new statement of the means and purposes of religion. Such a vital, fearless, and frank religion capable of furnishing adequate social goals and personal satisfactions may appear to many people as a complete break with the past. While this age does owe a vast debt to the traditional religions, it is none the less obvious that any religion that can hope to be a synthesizing and dynamic force for today must be shaped for the needs of this age. To establish such a religion is a major necessity of the present. It is a responsibility which rests upon this generation. We therefore affirm the following:

When mankind tries to define and interpret the means and purposes of religion, he is really attempting to determine for himself that which he will adhere to in the will and plan of God the Father. And, as such, upon their rejection of any literal Biblical truth they reject the One True Creator God and His simple message. This is open rebellion by a group of individuals that have decided to exalt themselves above that which is truly superior to themsevles. And, as we can see in the text of this paragraph above, humanists once again prove that they are not willing to change to meet the requirements of God as presented through His Word, instead they seek to be "dynamic" and "synthesizing" to meet the "needs" of humanity. These needs have already been met and prepared for, it is humanity that chooses to reject the preparations because they chose first to reject the Preparer.

FIRST: Religious humanists regard the universe as self-existing and not created.

Open and willful rejection of the Word of God, provided as a complete and literal history of all mankind has been involved in as a gift from God to man (II Tim 3:16).

SECOND: Humanism believes that man is a part of nature and that he has emerged as a result of a continuous process.

This is another way of communicating their amplification of evolution.

THIRD: Holding an organic view of life, humanists find that the traditional dualism of mind and body must be rejected.

Philosophically required in their rational thought process to continue to reject God and intelligent design.

FOURTH: Humanism recognizes that man's religious culture and civilization, as clearly depicted by anthropology and history, are the product of a gradual development due to his interaction with his natural environment and with his social heritage. The individual born into a particular culture is largely molded by that culture.

This is another way of communicating their amplification of evolution while marginalizing the value of individual family and cultural ties. This is the seed of one world globalism and the destruction of the importance of the nuclear family.

FIFTH: Humanism asserts that the nature of the universe depicted by modern science makes unacceptable any supernatural or cosmic guarantees of human values. Obviously humanism does not deny the possibility of realities as yet undiscovered, but it does insist that the way to determine the existence and value of any and all realities is by means of intelligent inquiry and by the assessment of their relations to human needs. Religion must formulate its hopes and plans in the light of the scientific spirit and method.

Amplifying human judgement and empirical wisdom above that which has already been communicated to mankind by the One True Creator God. They choose to reject absolute values so that they can usher in more "dynamic" values to meet the "needs" of the people. However, they overlook the simple fact that the needs of the people have already been met and all that is required is that the individual accept that which will satiate those needs.

SIXTH: We are convinced that the time has passed for theism, deism, modernism, and the several varieties of "new thought".

Another means of launching their attack upon the sovereignty of God and His plan. They reject Him and are using this document to state that point.

SEVENTH: Religion consists of those actions, purposes, and experiences which are humanly significant. Nothing human is alien to the religious. It includes labor, art, science, philosophy, love, friendship, recreation -- all that is in its degree expressive of intelligently satisfying human living. The distinction between the sacred and the secular can no longer be maintained.

In truth, there was never any distinction between the sacred and the secular. Every single thing a person does - every moment of their life - is a sacred act as it is either done by one who is reconciled eternally to God or they are in rebellion against him and will spend eternity in exile from Him. It is only the desire for an unbelieving mankind to ignore that fact that has allowed mankind to live in a delusion creating two different realms of action. This is, therefore, a strawman aflame. Labor, art, science, philosophy, love, friendship, recreation and all other events of life could not have come about without first the benevolent and true actions of the Father in eternity past.

EIGHTH: Religious Humanism considers the complete realization of human personality to be the end of man's life and seeks its development and fulfillment in the here and now. This is the explanation of the humanist's social passion.

Again, they amplify the value of humanity while rejecting the genuine purpose and true fulfillment of each human life. Another note... God provided mankind with the authority to exercise their volition. It is His gift that gives them the opportunity to reject Him.

NINTH: In the place of the old attitudes involved in worship and prayer the humanist finds his religious emotions expressed in a heightened sense of personal life and in a cooperative effort to promote social well-being.

Once again amplifying themselves and their agenda/desires over the will and plan of the Father. In the process, they intend to promote the rejection of the One True Creator God through their use of the word "religion". They replace the true of God with a lie, that lie is, of course, humanism. See Rom 1:25.

TENTH: It follows that there will be no uniquely religious emotions and attitudes of the kind hitherto associated with belief in the supernatural.

Yet another open salvo at the One True Creator God. This time, through their rejection of the transcendence of human improvement through spiritual submission to Him and His Word.

ELEVENTH: Man will learn to face the crises of life in terms of his knowledge of their naturalness and probability. Reasonable and manly attitudes will be fostered by education and supported by custom. We assume that humanism will take the path of social and mental hygiene and discourage sentimental and unreal hopes and wishful thinking.

Philosophical and psychological indoctrination preparation by those who wish to do the programming.

TWELFTH: Believing that religion must work increasingly for joy in living, religious humanists aim to foster the creative in man and to encourage achievements that add to the satisfactions of life.

Hedonism, amplifying the value of whatever feels good to the people, even if it is outside of the plan of God or is a distraction of/used by Satan.

THIRTEENTH: Religious humanism maintains that all associations and institutions exist for the fulfillment of human life. The intelligent evaluation, transformation, control, and direction of such associations and institutions with a view to the enhancement of human life is the purpose and program of humanism. Certainly religious institutions, their ritualistic forms, ecclesiastical methods, and communal activities must be reconstituted as rapidly as experience allows, in order to function effectively in the modern world.

The core of the action arm of the humanist movement is displayed here. Both their philosophy and mission statement are clearly presented. In summary; "By man, for man." is the order of the day. Forget God and His demands/desires for He does not exist in their estimation, or, if He does exist then He must bend His will to the will of mankind. Therefore, whatever man decrees (in the appearance of the "majority rules" mentality) is the order of the day. In the process, they have every intention of deconstructing all religions to burn at their sacrificial altar of humanity and they make an open admission of this fact.

FOURTEENTH: The humanists are firmly convinced that existing acquisitive and profit-motivated society has shown itself to be inadequate and that a radical change in methods, controls, and motives must be instituted. A socialized and cooperative economic order must be established to the end that the equitable distribution of the means of life be possible. The goal of humanism is a free and universal society in which people voluntarily and intelligently cooperate for the common good. Humanists demand a shared life in a shared world.

Here is their economic diatribe, stating open warfare against the economic systems of the socieites most individuals exist within, including all capitalist systems. While this author will admit that any monetary system will have flaws (I Tim 6:10), only adherence to God and His Word (literally presented and accepted) and the pressing forward to the goal of the genuine Christian life will prove to be the best approach to handling economies in this age that we live in. Any other approach will eventually be proven inadequate, flawed and even false.

FIFTEENTH AND LAST: We assert that humanism will: (a) affirm life rather than deny it; (b) seek to elicit the possibilities of life, not flee from them; and (c) endeavor to establish the conditions of a satisfactory life for all, not merely for the few. By this positive morale and intention humanism will be guided, and from this perspective and alignment the techniques and efforts of humanism will flow.

It is without question that some of the initial motivations of many of those who contributed to this document were "noble" and based in a desire to see improvement in society. Sadly, they decided that they had justification to disassemble the authority of God in the process. Instead of accepting the system God provided to meet the needs of mankin d and demanding that individual Christians adhere to that system, they reject God and throw him into the trash heap of humanist philosophy and the worship of mankind.

So stand the theses of religious humanism. Though we consider the religious forms and ideas of our fathers no longer adequate, the quest for the good life is still the central task for mankind. Man is at last becoming aware that he alone is responsible for the realization of the world of his dreams, that he has within himself the power for its achievement. He must set intelligence and will to the task.

"The quest for the good life" as alluded to above was never the genuine central task for mankind. Instead, the true central task of mankind is to first accept the reconciliation to God provided for by His offer of Jesus Christ and then to glorify Him by your submission to Him and His Word and the actions of ministry that come about as a result of that submission to Him. Since humanists refuse to acknowledge this universal and indisputable truth, they cannot ever truly be capable of solving the problems they seek to resolve.

Humanist Manifesto II (1973)

It is forty years since Humanist Manifesto I (1933) appeared. Events since then make that earlier statement seem far too optimistic. Nazism has shown the depths of brutality of which humanity is capable. Other totalitarian regimes have suppressed human rights without ending poverty. Science has sometimes brought evil as well as good. Recent decades have shown that inhuman wars can be made in the name of peace. The beginnings of police states, even in democratic societies, widespread government espionage, and other abuses of power by military, political, and industrial elites, and the continuance of unyielding racism, all present a different and difficult social outlook. In various societies, the demands of women and minority groups for equal rights effectively challenge our generation.

As we approach the twenty-first century, however, an affirmative and hopeful vision is needed. Faith, commensurate with advancing knowledge, is also necessary. In the choice between despair and hope, humanists respond in this Humanist Manifesto II with a positive declaration for times of uncertainty.

As in 1933, humanists still believe that traditional theism, especially faith in the prayer-hearing God, assumed to live and care for persons, to hear and understand their prayers, and to be able to do something about them, is an unproved and outmoded faith. Salvationism, based on mere affirmation, still appears as harmful, diverting people with false hopes of heaven hereafter. Reasonable minds look to other means for survival.

Those who sign Humanist Manifesto II disclaim that they are setting forth a binding credo; their individual views would be stated in widely varying ways. This statement is, however, reaching for vision in a time that needs direction. It is social analysis in an effort at consensus. New statements should be developed to supersede this, but for today it is our conviction that humanism offers an alternative that can serve present-day needs and guide humankind toward the future.

-- Paul Kurtz and Edwin H. Wilson (1973)

Kurtz and Wilson begin with this preamble to describe the events that have been manifested as many of the problems of an increasingly godless society. Yet, they attempt to communicate that further distance (and total rejection) from the One True Creator God of the Bible is necessary to resolve these listed ills. All of the listed manifestations provided in the preamble are a result of the exploitation of man against man and have nothing whatsoever to do with the actions of God, save for His blessed longsuffering which allows mankind to have the time to make the reasonable decision to submit to Him and His Word so that some may be reconciled to Him for all eternity through Jesus Christ (John 14:6) and His grace through faith in the Body of Christ.

The next century can be and should be the humanistic century. Dramatic scientific, technological, and ever-accelerating social and political changes crowd our awareness. We have virtually conquered the planet, explored the moon, overcome the natural limits of travel and communication; we stand at the dawn of a new age, ready to move farther into space and perhaps inhabit other planets. Using technology wisely, we can control our environment, conquer poverty, markedly reduce disease, extend our life-span, significantly modify our behavior, alter the course of human evolution and cultural development, unlock vast new powers, and provide humankind with unparalleled opportunity for achieving an abundant and meaningful life.

While mentioning human evolution, they demonstrate their doctrine that the human race is the only means by which mankind will achieve utopia. The challenge of humanist utopia is that it is a utopia based not upon God's will or even an individual desire, but the desire of the collective. The collective, or the leadership of said collective first defines what the problems are that will be addressed. In the process, the needs/desires of the few (or one) are steamrolled by the majority. Many of the goals they yearn to achieve (as seen above) may not be true concerns or may have vague definition (such as "modify our behavior"). These individuals have begun using unclear goals and ill-defined terminology to gain a borader spectrum of acceptance amongst the masses.

The future is, however, filled with dangers. In learning to apply the scientific method to nature and human life, we have opened the door to ecological damage, over-population, dehumanizing institutions, totalitarian repression, and nuclear and bio- chemical disaster. Faced with apocalyptic prophesies and doomsday scenarios, many flee in despair from reason and embrace irrational cults and theologies of withdrawal and retreat.

Traditional moral codes and newer irrational cults both fail to meet the pressing needs of today and tomorrow. False "theologies of hope" and messianic ideologies, substituting new dogmas for old, cannot cope with existing world realities. They separate rather than unite peoples.

Notice how the future they reference is filled with dangers that came about solely by utilizing the engineering of the humanist science program to supposedly SOLVE past problems. Yet, they will once again claim that evolution is the order of the day, that the natural order of things is to try, try again and that practice will make perfect. Give humanists enough time, control and financial freedom and they will solve all problems that they have defined as solvable problems. Of course, it might take 2 billion years or some such nonsense, though with modern technological, pharmaceutical, social, cultural and phycological inventions it might be only another few generations before they have everything prepared for control. However, who will be the ones doing the decision making onto the definition of control and, eventually, utopia? C.S. Lewis in the volume "The Abolition of Man" deals with this very question and the horrifying result of the collective empowered by science and licensed by the masses.

Notice also that the necessity to reject God is hammered home yet again. Anything "traditional" must be left behind to attain a greater collective good. If a person does not relinquish their hold on traditional morality they hold back society and support the repression of the collective. This makes a God fearing individual who turns solely to traditional methods, means and morality (as demonstrated by the Bible and the enlightenment of the Holy Spirit) to solve their problems or to minister to and council others enemies of the collective and the state in the developed mentality of a humanist.

To begin to recognize the mentality of those waxing in our time, read through II Peter and find which statements could be attributed to humanists, friends, neighbors and coworkers today and in the future. Here is but one example:

"Beloved, I now write to you this second epistle (in both of which I stir up your pure minds by way of reminder), that you may

be mindful of the words which were spoken before by the holy prophets, and of the commandment of us, the apostles of the Lord and Savior, knowing this first: that scoffers will come in the last days, walking according to their own lusts, and saying, "Where is the promise of His coming? For since the fathers fell asleep, all things continue as they were from the beginning of creation." For this they willfully forget: that by the word of God the heavens were of old, and the earth standing out of water and in the water, by which the world that then existed perished, being flooded with water. But the heavens and the earth which are now preserved by the same word, are reserved for fire until the day of judgment and perdition of ungodly men. But, beloved, do not forget this one thing, that with the Lord one day is as a thousand years, and a thousand years as one day. The Lord is not slack concerning His promise, as some count slackness, but is longsuffering toward us, not willing that any should perish but that all should come to repentance." 2 Peter 3:1-9, NKJV.

Humanity, to survive, requires bold and daring measures. We need to extend the uses of scientific method, not renounce them, to fuse reason with compassion in order to build constructive social and moral values. Confronted by many possible futures, we must decide which to pursue. The ultimate goal should be the fulfillment of the potential for growth in each human personality -- not for the favored few, but for all of humankind. Only a shared world and global measures will suffice.

A humanist outlook will tap the creativity of each human being and provide the vision and courage for us to work together. This outlook emphasizes the role human beings can play in their own spheres of action. The decades ahead call for dedicated, clearminded men and women able to marshal the will, intelligence, and cooperative skills for shaping a desirable future. Humanism can provide the purpose and inspiration that so many seek; it can give personal meaning and significance to human life.

Only a genuine faith in the One True Creator God can provide the purpose and inspiration mankind truly needs to find personal meaning and significance to human life. This genuine faith is not the product of any single church or major denomination., It is by grace through faith alone in the Lord Jesus Christ. The humanist outlook is a diabolical distraction to pull humanity away from their true rescue and into the arms of destruction, a destruction that is job number one for Satan.

Many kinds of humanism exist in the contemporary world. The varieties and emphases of naturalistic humanism include "scientific," "ethical," "democratic," "religious," and "Marxist" humanism. Free thought, atheism, agnosticism, skepticism, deism, rationalism, ethical culture, and liberal religion all claim to be heir to the humanist tradition. Humanism traces its roots from ancient China, classical Greece and Rome, through the Renaissance and the Enlightenment, to the scientific revolution of the modern world. But views that merely reject theism are not equivalent to humanism. They lack commitment to the positive belief in the possibilities of human progress and to the values central to it. Many within religious groups, believing in the future of humanism, now claim humanist credentials. Humanism is an ethical process through which we all can move, above and beyond the divisive particulars, heroic personalities, dogmatic creeds, and ritual customs of past religions or their mere negation.

Notice the inclusion of that old adversary, liberal religion, as covered prior in this volume. Also, recognize that a rejection of God alone is not enough for the indoctrination for the humanist utopia to come. You must also accept and celebrate the value of mankind as sole controllers of their destiny and masters of their condition. You must worship humanity.

We affirm a set of common principles that can serve as a basis for united action -- positive principles relevant to the present human condition. They are a design for a secular society on a planetary scale.

Humanist Globalism, one of the end times prophecies of the Bible.

For these reasons, we submit this new Humanist Manifesto for the future of humankind; for us, it is a vision of hope, a direction for satisfying survival.

As soon as I read this I was reminded of the following verses:

""The thief does not come except to steal, and to kill, and to destroy. I have come that they may have life, and that they may have it more abundantly. "I am the good shepherd. The good shepherd gives His life for the sheep." John 10:10, 11, NKJV.

It is not difficult to see that we no longer need a vision of hope, a direction for satisfying survival due to the actions of the Lord Jesus Christ over 2,000 years ago. What we need is to accept these truths individually and demand that the corporate church take meaningful action based upon the literal understanding of and approach to the Bible.

-- Religion --

FIRST: In the best sense, religion may inspire dedication to the highest ethical ideals. The cultivation of moral devotion and creative imagination is an expression of genuine "spiritual" experience and aspiration.

They alter the true definition of spiritual above. They also do that which so many do, they confuse religion with true spirituality in Christ Jesus.

We believe, however, that traditional dogmatic or authoritarian religions that place revelation, God, ritual, or creed above human needs and experience do a disservice to the human species. Any account of nature should pass the tests of scientific evidence; in our judgment, the dogmas and myths of traditional religions do not do so. Even at this late date in human history, certain elementary facts based upon the critical use of scientific reason have to be restated. We find insufficient evidence for belief in the existence of a supernatural; it is either meaningless or irrelevant to the question of survival and fulfillment of the human race. As nontheists, we begin with humans not God, nature not deity. Nature may indeed be broader and deeper than we now know; any new discoveries, however, will but enlarge our knowledge of the natural.

Those who crafted and endorsed this document (Humanist Manifesto II) openly reject the One True Creator God who alone is sovereign and capable to determine that which is truth, moral and just. They must do this to continue on in their delusion of grandeur. While rejecting God they amplify mankind into the position of deity.

Some humanists believe we should reinterpret traditional religions and reinvest them with meanings appropriate to the current situation. Such redefinitions, however, often perpetuate old dependencies and escapisms; they easily become obscurantist, impeding the free use of the intellect. We need, instead, radically new human purposes and goals.

We appreciate the need to preserve the best ethical teachings in the religious traditions of humankind, many of which we share in common. But we reject those features of traditional religious morality that deny humans a full appreciation of their own potentialities and responsibilities. Traditional religions often offer solace to humans, but, as often, they inhibit humans from helping themselves or experiencing their full potentialities. Such institutions, creeds, and rituals often impede the will to serve others. Too often traditional faiths encourage dependence rather than independence, obedience rather than affirmation, fear rather than courage. More recently they have generated concerned social action, with many signs of relevance appearing in the wake of the "God Is Dead" theologies. But we can discover no divine purpose or providence for the human species. While there is much that we do not know, humans are responsible for what we are or will become. No deity will save us; we must save ourselves.

As they are not spiritual, they cannot accept the wisdom of God:

"For the wisdom of this world is foolishness with God. For it is written, "He catches the wise in their own craftiness"; and again, "The LORD knows the thoughts of the wise, that they are futile."" 1 *Corinthians 3:19, 20, NKJV.*

As a result, they will be frustrated time and again until God finally ends their open rebellion.

SECOND: Promises of immortal salvation or fear of eternal damnation are both illusory and harmful. They distract humans from present concerns, from self-actualization, and from rectifying social injustices. Modern science discredits such historic concepts as the "ghost in the machine" and the "separable soul." Rather, science affirms that the human species is an emergence from natural evolutionary forces. As far as we know, the total personality is a function of the biological organism transacting in a social and cultural context. There is no credible evidence that life survives the death of the body. We continue to exist in our progeny and in the way that our lives have influenced others in our culture.

Science has proven that there is no such thing as eternal salvation, or so they claim above. However, of course science cannot prove this, all science and humanism can do is deny this, which they do early and often. Of course, they then need to redefine the term "exist" so that they can apply it in a death defying context. Yes, portions of our DNA might continue to be present in the DNA structure of our offspring, and certain portions of some limited memories may as well, but the human parent of a child no longer truly exists once they die a physical death. Nor does the full and deeply personal experience or spiritual responsibility of each individual pass along to any other person. It is impossible to use science to prove or disprove the reality of the soul. The soul is spiritual, given solely by God (and owned completely and totally only by Him) and beyond full human comprehension in this present age. Modern science is based in the worship of the research and humanity and is thereby incapable of recognizing spiritual truths.

Traditional religions are surely not the only obstacles to human progress. Other ideologies also impede human advance. Some forms of political doctrine, for instance, function religiously, reflecting the worst features of orthodoxy and authoritarianism, especially when they sacrifice individuals on the altar of Utopian promises. Purely economic and political viewpoints, whether capitalist or communist, often function as religious and ideological dogma. Although humans undoubtedly need economic and political goals, they also need creative values by which to live.

And here they throw in their all-encompassing passage on the need for all pursuits outside of "religion" to submit to their new order of things (humanism).

-- Ethics --

THIRD: We affirm that moral values derive their source from human experience. Ethics is autonomous and situational needing no theological or ideological sanction. Ethics stems from human need and interest. To deny this distorts the whole basis of life. Human life has meaning because we create and develop our futures. Happiness and the creative realization of human needs and desires, individually and in shared enjoyment, are continuous themes of humanism. We strive for the good life, here and now. The goal is to pursue life's enrichment despite debasing forces of vulgarization, commercialization, and dehumanization.

Since God does not exist in the delusional mind of a humanist, they can then "rationally" reject the necessity of His abolsutle authority and judgement. This fits their needs well as they cannot accept a set of moral absolutes without compromising their developing plan of action. Satan cannot proceed with his diabolical plan if mankind recognizes the authority of God.

FOURTH: Reason and intelligence are the most effective instruments that humankind possesses. There is no substitute: neither faith nor passion suffices in itself. The controlled use of scientific

95

methods, which have transformed the natural and social sciences since the Renaissance, must be extended further in the solution of human problems. But reason must be tempered by humility, since no group has a monopoly of wisdom or virtue. Nor is there any guarantee that all problems can be solved or all questions answered. Yet critical intelligence, infused by a sense of human caring, is the best method that humanity has for resolving problems. Reason should be balanced with compassion and empathy and the whole person fulfilled. Thus, we are not advocating the use of scientific intelligence independent of or in opposition to emotion, for we believe in the cultivation of feeling and love. As science pushes back the boundary of the known, humankind's sense of wonder is continually renewed, and art, poetry, and music find their places, along with religion and ethics.

The first sentence is mainly accurate for the life of an unbeliever. If a person rejects the instrument of the Gospel of Christ then they cannot be given further spiritual enlightenment into the truth of the Word and are then logically and intellectually hamstrung by their own rejection. Most unbelievers are under the impression that their concerns are genuine concerns of God, which is not always the case. Most unbelievers also believe that their concerns in any of thousands of different perceived situations will be the impetus that causes God to act. And, if an unbeliever determines through their perception that God has not resolved the situation that brought about their concern, they reject Him more strongly than before. Compassion, feeling and love are all emotions placed within us by our One True Creator God and will never be fully embraced or channeled unless one submits to Him who created those emotional responses. Briefly notice how they contend that science will put religion into its proper place; in the incinerator of humanism and historically nothing more than as a proverbial speedbump hampering the joys of a utopian collective.

"But even if our gospel is veiled, it is veiled to those who are perishing, whose minds the god of this age has blinded, who do not believe, lest the light of the gospel of the glory of Christ, who is the image of God, should shine on them." 2 Corinthians 4:3, 4, NKJV.

-- The Individual --

FIFTH: The preciousness and dignity of the individual person is a central humanist value. Individuals should be encouraged to realize their own creative talents and desires. We reject all religious, ideological, or moral codes that denigrate the individual, suppress freedom, dull intellect, dehumanize personality. We believe in maximum individual autonomy consonant with social responsibility. Although science can account for the causes of behavior, the possibilities of individual freedom of choice exist in human life and should be increased.

Since humanists reject God and absolute truth, they then can (and must) reject the concept of sin. The hoi polloi like this tenant of humanism perhaps best of all. The only responsibility for a humanist collective society is that which is considered "socially responsible". The term "socially responsible" is another way to cause one to accept moral evolution coupled with situational ethics. The principle problem with the evolution of morality is that it keeps morality in flux and can be altered at any time upon the wishes of whomever has the power to enforce the new morality. Yet, without acceptance of the Sovereign God, they cannot have anything solid to base morality upon. Eventually, this morality practiced by humanists will manifest itself as a means to encourage solely depraved behavior by mankind as Satan wishes mankind to reject all genuine truths (since God created all truth and Satan is in diametrical opposition to anything God has declared "good").

SIXTH: In the area of sexuality, we believe that intolerant attitudes, often cultivated by orthodox religions and puritanical cultures, unduly repress sexual conduct. The right to birth control, abortion, and divorce should be recognized. While we do not approve of exploitive, denigrating forms of sexual expression, neither do we wish to prohibit, by law or social sanction, sexual behavior between consenting adults. The many varieties of sexual exploration should not in themselves be considered "evil." Without countenancing mindless permissiveness or unbridled promiscuity, a civilized society should be a tolerant one. Short of harming others or compelling them to do likewise, individuals should be permitted to express their sexual proclivities and pursue their life-styles as they desire. We wish to cultivate the development of a responsible attitude toward sexuality, in which humans are not exploited as sexual objects, and in which intimacy, sensitivity, respect, and honesty in interpersonal relations are encouraged. Moral education for children and adults is an important way of developing awareness and sexual maturity.

Simply put, the vast bulk of this entire passage is simply placed here as a result of the humanist amplification of a sinful life devoid of Godliness while embracing their worship of the human experience and existentialism. Of course they have no holds barred as they assume themselves to be the only means by which morality can be developed and judged. As an aside, this passage would have to be included in a society in which moral evolution is the order of the day. Remember the term "socially responsible"? At the time that the document preparers worked on Humanist Manifesto II, there was a significant social movement towards the validation of the sexual revolution. One day, if they remain true to their socially responsible morality standpoint humanists might be forced to alter this language to better reflect the changing social responsibilities of the future. In other words, if the majority wish for a specific set of socially acceptable standards that runs counter to these protections and prohibitions then the morality listed above would be forced to change with the winds of society. Without absolute morality there can be no absolute value of human lives or rights.

-- Democratic Society --

SEVENTH: To enhance freedom and dignity the individual must experience a full range of civil liberties in all societies. This includes freedom of speech and the press, political democracy, the legal right of opposition to governmental policies, fair judicial process, religious liberty, freedom of association, and artistic, scientific, and cultural freedom. It also includes a recognition of an individual's right to die with dignity, euthanasia, and the right to suicide. We oppose the increasing invasion of privacy, by whatever means, in both totalitarian and democratic societies. We would safeguard, extend, and implement the principles of human freedom evolved from the Magna Carta to the Bill of Rights, the Rights of Man, and the Universal Declaration of Human Rights.

EIGHTH: We are committed to an open and democratic society. We must extend participatory democracy in its true sense to the economy, the school, the family, the workplace, and voluntary associations. Decision-making must be decentralized to include widespread involvement of people at all levels -- social, political, and economic. All persons should have a voice in developing the values and goals that determine their lives. Institutions should be responsive to expressed desires and needs. The conditions of work, education,

98

devotion, and play should be humanized. Alienating forces should be modified or eradicated and bureaucratic structures should be held to a minimum. People are more important than decalogues, rules, proscriptions, or regulations.

Most of the concepts in section eight above are already provided for in the Word of God. And, should unbelievers become true believers and practice the truths of the Bible they would find that conditions of work, education, devotion and play would be more than humanized, they would be Biblicized. Eventually, however, every society must submit to the Lord Jesus Christ (Philippians 2:9-11) and not to the humanist collective.

One of the more disconcerting portions found above concerns the "alienating forces". Who determines what those alienating forces are and how they will be modified or eradicated? ALl of this is foolishness to God, who alone is qualified to rule over not only humanity but His entire created universe.

NINTH: The separation of church and state and the separation of ideology and state are imperatives. The state should encourage maximum freedom for different moral, political, religious, and social values in society. It should not favor any particular religious bodies through the use of public monies, nor espouse a single ideology and function thereby as an instrument of propaganda or oppression, particularly against dissenters.

This is put in place largely to continue an indoctrination of rejecting God.

TENTH: Humane societies should evaluate economic systems not by rhetoric or ideology, but by whether or not they increase economic well-being for all individuals and groups, minimize poverty and hardship, increase the sum of human satisfaction, and enhance the quality of life. Hence the door is open to alternative economic systems. We need to democratize the economy and judge it by its responsiveness to human needs, testing results in terms of the common good.

As I communicated above, here is another economic diatribe, stating open warfare against the economic systems of the socieites most individuals exist within, including all capitalist systems. While this author will admit that any monetary system will have flaws (I Tim 6:10), only adherence to God and His Word (literally presented and accepted) and the pressing forward to the goal of the genuine

Christian life will prove to be the best approach to handling economies in this age that we live in. Any other approach will eventually be proven inadequate, flawed and even false. The most obvious flaw in section ten, above, must deal directly with how one defines "human need" and draw the line between "need" and want/desire while also defining the "common good". Who will be entrusted to make these distinctions?

ELEVENTH: The principle of moral equality must be furthered through elimination of all discrimination based upon race, religion, sex, age, or national origin. This means equality of opportunity and recognition of talent and merit. Individuals should be encouraged to contribute to their own betterment. If unable, then society should provide means to satisfy their basic economic, health, and cultural needs, including, wherever resources make possible, a minimum guaranteed annual income. We are concerned for the welfare of the aged, the infirm, the disadvantaged, and also for the outcasts -- the mentally retarded, abandoned, or abused children, the handicapped, prisoners, and addicts -- for all who are neglected or ignored by society. Practicing humanists should make it their vocation to humanize personal relations.

God already provided for these protections amongst His children (true believers in Christ alone):

"There is neither Jew nor Greek, there is neither slave nor free, there is neither male nor female; for you are all one in Christ Jesus." Galatians 3:28, NKJV.

The epistles of the Apostle Paul as well as the words of Jesus Christ in the gospels all demonstrate repeatedly that the infirm, the aged, the abused, the least of all men should be protected and supported whenever possible. The problem is not that Christianity does not have the commandment and the instructions or empowerment. The problem is that liberal Christianity has eclipsed true spirituality and is intentionally leading mankind away from the truths and values of the Word. This is Satan's plan and mankind endorses that plan, by and large.

We believe in the right to universal education. Everyone has a right to the cultural opportunity to fulfill his or her unique capacities and talents. The schools should foster satisfying and productive living. They should be open at all levels to any and all; the achievement of excellence should be encouraged. Innovative and

100

experimental forms of education are to be welcomed. The energy and idealism of the young deserve to be appreciated and channeled to constructive purposes.

Here are more vague concepts to encourage the support of the public. Anything less than a Biblically based education respecting traditional morality and teaching the truths of the Holy Bible, rightly divided, will be less than ideal. If that can be accomplished on a universal scale in this age, then many aspects of living would be improved exponentially.

We deplore racial, religious, ethnic, or class antagonisms. Although we believe in cultural diversity and encourage racial and ethnic pride, we reject separations which promote alienation and set people and groups against each other; we envision an integrated community where people have a maximum opportunity for free and voluntary association.

God already provided for these protections amongst His children (true believers in Christ alone):

"There is neither Jew nor Greek, there is neither slave nor free, there is neither male nor female; for you are all one in Christ Jesus." Galatians 3:28, NKJV.

Also, Galatians and I Corinthians clearly demonstrate the behavior Christians are instructed to practice daily:

"But the fruit of the Spirit is love, joy, peace, longsuffering, kindness, goodness, faithfulness, gentleness, self-control. Against such there is no law." Galatians 5:22, 23, NKJV.

"Love suffers long and is kind; love does not envy; love does not parade itself, is not puffed up; does not behave rudely, does not seek its own, is not provoked, thinks no evil; does not rejoice in iniquity, but rejoices in the truth; bears all things, believes all things, hopes all things, endures all things. Love never fails..." 1 Corinthians 13:4-8, NKJV.

In short, racial tensions are a diabolical invention of Satan and a sinful humanity (there is not now and there has not been any basis for racial segregation of any kind since the days of the Apostle Paul as he eliminates any debate about racial differences in the eyes of God in his epistles). Racial divisions are intended to create discontent and mistrust amongst mankind and away from the glorification of God. They are a tool of Satan.

We are critical of sexism or sexual chauvinism -- male or female. We believe in equal rights for both women and men to fulfill their unique careers and potentialities as they see fit, free of invidious discrimination.

Since humanists reject God and His Word, they cannot accept the DIFFERENT and COMPLIMENTARY roles of men and women as uniquely designed. Most of the dysfunctions in our modern societies are due mainly to the rejection of these traditional successfully applied values of the Bible. Ephesians chapters five and six provide many of the necessary guidelines for interpersonal respect and healthy concern for interpersonal relationships.

Also, Galatians and I Corinthians clearly demonstrate the behavior Christians are instructed to practice daily:

"But the fruit of the Spirit is love, joy, peace, longsuffering, kindness, goodness, faithfulness, gentleness, self-control. Against such there is no law." Galatians 5:22, 23, NKJV.

"Love suffers long and is kind; love does not envy; love does not parade itself, is not puffed up; does not behave rudely, does not seek its own, is not provoked, thinks no evil; does not rejoice in iniquity, but rejoices in the truth; bears all things, believes all things, hopes all things, endures all things. Love never fails..." 1 Corinthians 13:4-8, NKJV.

There is a recognized difference between respecting the will and plan of God as designed by Him and the will and plans of a God rejecting individual. Simply because a person may wish to be treated a certain way does not mean that they are entitled to be treated outside of the rights that God provided to them. We should treat all people as God would treat them as outlined in the Word.

-- World Community --

TWELFTH: We deplore the division of humankind on nationalistic grounds. We have reached a turning point in human history where the best option is to transcend the limits of national sovereignty and to move toward the building of a world community in which all sectors of the human family can participate. Thus we look to the development of a system of world law and a world order based upon transnational federal government. This would appreciate cultural pluralism and diversity. It would not exclude pride in national origins and accomplishments nor the handling of regional problems on a regional basis. Human progress, however, can no longer be achieved by focusing on one section of the world, Western or Eastern, developed or underdeveloped. For the first time in human history, no part of humankind can be isolated from any other. Each person's future is in some way linked to all. We thus reaffirm a commitment to the building of world community, at the same time recognizing that this commits us to some hard choices.

Humanist Globalism, one of the end times prophecies of the Bible.

THIRTEENTH: This world community must renounce the resort to violence and force as a method of solving international disputes. We believe in the peaceful adjudication of differences by international courts and by the development of the arts of negotiation and compromise. War is obsolete. So is the use of nuclear, biological, and chemical weapons. It is a planetary imperative to reduce the level of military expenditures and turn these savings to peaceful and people-oriented uses.

"For you yourselves know perfectly that the day of the Lord so comes as a thief in the night. For when they say, "Peace and safety!" then sudden destruction comes upon them, as labor pains upon a pregnant woman. And they shall not escape." 1 Thessalonians 5:2, 3, NKJV.

FOURTEENTH: The world community must engage in cooperative planning concerning the use of rapidly depleting resources. The planet earth must be considered a single ecosystem. Ecological damage, resource depletion, and excessive population growth must be checked by international concord. The cultivation and conservation of nature is a moral value; we should perceive ourselves as integral to the sources of our being in nature. We must free our world from needless pollution and waste, responsibly guarding and creating wealth, both natural and human. Exploitation of natural resources, uncurbed by social conscience, must end.

There is much debate and emphasis placed upon "global warming" and "climate change" in our modern society. This is a distraction away from God and His glory as engineered by Satan and a humanity increasingly in opposition to the Lord (and increasingly embracing humanism).

*""While the earth remains, Seedtime and harvest, Cold and heat, Winter and summer, And day and night Shall not cease.""
Genesis 8:22, NKJV.*

God created the world:

"For by Him all things were created that are in heaven and that are on earth, visible and invisible, whether thrones or dominions or principalities or powers. All things were created through Him and for Him." Colossians 1:16, NKJV.

God owns His creation:

"<<A Psalm of David.>> The earth is the LORD'S, and all its fullness, The world and those who dwell therein." Psalms 24:1, NKJV.

We who respect God should treat His creation with the respect it deserves while adhering to the Word, rightly divided.

FIFTEENTH: The problems of economic growth and development can no longer be resolved by one nation alone; they are worldwide in scope. It is the moral obligation of the developed nations to provide -- through an international authority that safeguards human rights -- massive technical, agricultural, medical, and economic assistance, including birth control techniques, to the developing portions of the globe. World poverty must cease. Hence extreme disproportions in wealth, income, and economic growth should be reduced on a worldwide basis.

Humanist Globalism, one of the end times prophecies of the Bible. See Rev. 13:16,17 specifically for economic requirements of Satan in the end-times.

SIXTEENTH: Technology is a vital key to human progress and development. We deplore any neo-romantic efforts to condemn indiscriminately all technology and science or to counsel retreat from its further extension and use for the good of humankind. We would resist any moves to censor basic scientific research on moral, political, or social grounds. Technology must, however, be carefully judged by the consequences of its use; harmful and destructive changes should be avoided. We are particularly disturbed when technology and bureaucracy control, manipulate, or modify human beings without their consent. Technological feasibility does not imply social or cultural desirability.

See chapter 13 of this volume.

SEVENTEENTH: We must expand communication and transportation across frontiers. Travel restrictions must cease. The world must be open to diverse political, ideological, and moral viewpoints and evolve a worldwide system of television and radio for information and education. We thus call for full international cooperation in culture, science, the arts, and technology across ideological borders. We must learn to live openly together or we shall perish together.

Humanist Globalism, one of the end times prophecies of the Bible. Along the way, as already communicated in previous chapters of this volume, there will be stages of social government, namely socialism and communism as Satan and a God rejecting humanity welcomes this humanist globalism.

-- Humanity As a Whole --

IN CLOSING: The world cannot wait for a reconciliation of competing political or economic systems to solve its problems. These are the times for men and women of goodwill to further the building of a peaceful and prosperous world. We urge that parochial loyalties and inflexible moral and religious ideologies be transcended. We urge recognition of the common humanity of all people. We further urge the use of reason and compassion to produce the kind of world we want -- a world in which peace, prosperity, freedom, and happiness are widely shared. Let us not abandon that vision in despair or cowardice. We are responsible for what we are or will be. Let us work together for a humane world by means commensurate with humane ends. Destructive ideological differences among communism, capitalism, socialism, conservatism, liberalism, and radicalism should be overcome. Let us call for an end to terror and hatred. We will survive and prosper only in a world of shared humane values. We can initiate new directions for humankind; ancient rivalries can be superseded by broad-based cooperative efforts. The commitment to tolerance, understanding, and peaceful negotiation does not necessitate acquiescence to the status quo nor the damming up of dynamic and revolutionary forces. The true revolution is occurring and can continue in countless nonviolent adjustments. But this entails the willingness to step forward onto new and expanding plateaus. At the present juncture of history, commitment to all humankind is the highest commitment of which we are capable; it transcends the narrow allegiances of church, state, party, class, or race in moving toward a wider vision of human potentiality. What more daring a goal for humankind than for each person to become, in ideal as well as practice, a citizen of a world community. It is a classical vision; we can now give it new vitality. Humanism thus interpreted is a moral force that has time on its side. We believe that humankind has the potential, intelligence, goodwill, and cooperative skill to implement this commitment in the decades ahead.

We, the undersigned, while not necessarily endorsing every detail of the above, pledge our general support to Humanist Manifesto II for the future of humankind. These affirmations are not a final credo or dogma but an expression of a living and growing faith. We invite others in all lands to join us in further developing and working for these goals.

Humanism is exalted here as a means to transcend the negative social state of humanity. However, through their amplification of human worship and their distancing from the truth of God, Jesus Christ and our living hope as individuals in this world, they leave us without eternal value or meaning and guide unbelievers into eternal destruction and separation from Him.

Humanist Manifesto 2000 (2000)

1. Preamble

Humanism is an ethical, scientific, and philosophical outlook that has changed the world. Its heritage traces back to the philosophers and poets of ancient Greece and Rome, Confucian China, and the Charvaka movement in classical India. Humanist artists, writers, scientists, and thinkers have been shaping the modern era for over half a millennium. Indeed, humanism and modernism have often seemed synonymous for humanist ideas and values express a renewed confidence in the power of human beings to solve their own problems and conquer uncharted frontiers.

This section really only serves to demonstrate the failed solutions of humanism and its components as demonstrated by centuries of suffering continued social tinkering. It is true that humanism has changed the world (and will continue to do so), but it has been nothing more than a diabolical distraction from the true solution to the problems of mankind, Christ crucified and resurrected for the benefit of all mankind. Instead of adhering to reality and the truth, humanists reject the Word as provided to us and simply claim it all to be erroneous. They do this as they are in competition to the truth and the glory of God as instructed and developed by Satan.

""How you are fallen from heaven, O Lucifer, son of the morning! How you are cut down to the ground, You who weakened the nations! For you have said in your heart: 'I will ascend into heaven, I will exalt my throne above the stars of God; I will also sit on the mount of the congregation On the farthest sides of the north; I will ascend above the heights of the clouds, I will be like the Most High.'" Isaiah 14:12-14, NKJV.

II. Prospects for a Better Future

For the first time in human history we possess the means provided by science and technology to ameliorate the human condition, advance happiness and freedom, and enhance human life for all people on this planet.

See hapter 13.

III. Scientific Naturalism

The unique message of humanism on the current world scene is its commitment to scientific naturalism. Most world views accepted today are spiritual, mystical, or theological in character. They have their origins in ancient pre-urban, nomadic, and agricultural societies of the past, not in the modern industrial or postindustrial global information culture that is emerging. Scientific naturalism enables human beings to construct a coherent world view disentangled from metaphysics or theology and based on the sciences.

The writer(s) of this manifesto obviously hold to the erroneous belief that those in previous centuries were not intellectual, or at least were not rationally competitive when compared to the "brilliant" minds of today. Humanists also often confuse technology development and use with intelligence or mental capacity. And, to those who do so, transceding intelligence (as defined by them) equates to superiority. However, as "enabling" as the realm of scientific naturalism might be to constructing God rejecting world-views, it is not cohesive when really looked at in depth and detail. Instead, scientific naturalism really just allows more fallacy based upon the flawed philosophy of evolution.

IV. The Benefits of Technology

Humanists have consistently defended the beneficent values of scientific technology for human welfare. Philosophers from Francis Bacon to John Dewey have emphasized the increased power over nature that scientific knowledge affords and how it can contribute immeasurably to human advancement and happiness.

See chapter 13.

V. Ethics and Reason

The realization of the highest ethical values is essential to the humanist outlook. We believe that growth of scientific knowledge will enable humans to make wiser choices. In this way there is no impenetrable wall between fact and value, is and ought. Using reason and cognition will better enable us to appraise our values in the light of evidence and by their consequences.

The good news for the writer(s) of sevtion five, above, is that these ethical values can be discovered today and without the use of expensive or deifficult to utilize technolgy. These values they are searching for will be found solely in the Word of God, rightly divided.

VI. A Universal Commitment to Humanity as a Whole

The overriding need of the world community today is to develop a new Planetary Humanism—one that seeks to preserve human rights and enhance human freedom and dignity, but also emphasizes our commitment to humanity as a whole. The underlying ethical principle of Planetary Humanism is the need to respect the dignity and worth of all persons in the world community.

God already provided for these protections amongst His children (true believers in Christ alone):

"There is neither Jew nor Greek, there is neither slave nor free, there is neither male nor female; for you are all one in Christ Jesus." Galatians 3:28, NKJV.

Also, Galatians and I Corinthians clearly demonstrate the behavior Christians are instructed to practice daily:

"But the fruit of the Spirit is love, joy, peace, longsuffering, kindness, goodness, faithfulness, gentleness, self-control. Against such there is no law." Galatians 5:22, 23, NKJV.

"Love suffers long and is kind; love does not envy; love does not parade itself, is not puffed up; does not behave rudely, does not seek its own, is not provoked, thinks no evil; does not rejoice in iniquity, but rejoices in the truth; bears all things, believes all things, hopes all things, endures all things. Love never fails..." 1 Corinthians 13:4-8, NKJV.

In short, racial tensions are a diabolical invention of Satan and a sinful humanity (there is not now and there has not been any basis for racial segregation of any kind since the days of the Apostle Paul as he eliminates any debate about racial differences in the eyes of God in his epistles). Racial divisions are intended to create discontent and mistrust amongst mankind and away from the glorification of God. They are a tool of Satan.

VII. A Planetary Bill of Rights and Responsibilities

To fulfill our commitment to Planetary Humanism, we offer a Planetary Bill of Rights and Responsibilities, which embodies our planetary commitment to the well-being of humanity as a whole. It incorporates the Universal Declaration of Human Rights, but goes beyond it by offering some new provisions. Many independent countries have sought to implement these provisions within their own national borders. But there is a growing need for an explicit Planetary Bill of Rights and Responsibilities that applies to all members of the human species.

See annotation on section six, above. That global imperative already exists in the Bible and does not need improvement. All that is required is the implementation of the Word of God in the lives of those who have submitted themselves to His will and program.

VIII. A New Global Agenda

Many of the high ideals that emerged following the Second World War, and that found expression in such instruments as the Universal Declaration of Human Rights, have waned through the world. If we are to influence the future of humankind, we will need to work increasingly with and through the new centers of power and influence to improve equity and stability, alleviate poverty, reduce conflict, and safeguard the environment.

"You never let a serious crisis go to waste. And what I mean by that it's an opprotunity to do things you think you could not do before." – Rahm Emanuel, former White House Chief of Staff under President Obama

To suggest that power and authority in a crisis should be used to promote a global agenda while indoctrinating (or, "influencing" as found above) individuals and engineering the future of humanity is an anti-Biblical mindset. It is a mindest that works agains tthe sovereignty of God while flexing the muscle of humanity against His will.

The mere title of this section requires me to once again also mention humanist globalism, one of the end times prophecies of the Bible.

IX. The Need for New Planetary Institutions

The urgent question in the twenty-first century is whether humankind can develop global institutions to address these problems. Many of the best remedies are those adopted on the local, national, and regional level by voluntary, private, and public efforts. One strategy is to seek solutions through free-market initiatives; another is to use international voluntary foundations and organizations for educational and social development. We believe, however, that there remains a need to develop new global institutions that will deal with the problems directly and will focus on the needs of humanity as a whole. These include the call for a bicameral legislature in the United Nations, with a World Parliament elected by the people, an income tax to help the underdeveloped countries, the end of the veto in the

Security Council, an environmental agency, and a world court with powers of enforcement.

Humanist Globalism, one of the end times prophecies of the Bible. The culimation of almost every humanist's dreams is outlined in the above section. Nowhere does it recognize the sovereignty of the One True Creator God.

X. Optimism about the Human Prospect

Finally, and perhaps most importantly, as members of the human community on this planet we need to nurture a sense of optimism about the human prospect. Although many problems may seem intractable, we have good reasons to believe that we can marshal our talent to solve them, and that by goodwill and dedication a better life will be attainable by more and more members of the human community. Planetary humanism holds forth great promises for humankind. We wish to cultivate a sense of wonder and excitement about the potential opportunities for realizing enriched lives for ourselves and for generations yet to be born.

Humanity is born into sin and all good things we do as unbelievers are but waste and shame to God (Romans 5:12, Romans 3:20-23, Isaiah. 64:6). This is the outlook of God. Instead of amplifying humanity, we should submit ourselves to God and take advantage of His gift of Christ:

"There is therefore now no condemnation to those who are in Christ Jesus, who do not walk according to the flesh, but according to the Spirit. For the law of the Spirit of life in Christ Jesus has made me free from the law of sin and death." Romans 8:1, 2, NKJV.

To solve (or at least mitigate) some of the social issues of humanity you must first believe in the Lord Jesus Christ, turn that belief into learning about His Word, rightly divided and amplify His Word increasingly in your life while living that ministry first to yourself and then unto others. Humanism, of any kind or type will do nothing more than march men further along the road to perdition and eternal separation from God and His children. Humanism is a tool of Satan, developed to distract mankind from the truth.

Become enthusiastic about the wonder and excitement of the truth of the Word! Turn to God and depend solely upon that which He has provided for you in this age; the Bible, the empowering Holy

Spirit (both of which will always be in full agreement, there is no new revelation from the Spirit that would conflict with the Word) and fellowship with other true believers. He will be ushering in the next stages of His program soon, use this time of His longsuffering to enrich and educate yourselves and generation yet to come.

Appendix II

Further reading and research:

To expound upon the subjects mentioned or detailed in this volume, the author would suggest the following resources (books listed first, online resources & hands on opportunities follow):

Title: The Holy Bible
Version: Choose a literal word for word translation whenever possible.

Title: 7 Men Who Rule the World from the Grave
Author: Dave Breese
ISBN (10): 0802484484

Title: The New Answers Book: Over 25 Questions on Creation / Evolution and the Bible
Author: Ken Ham
ISBN (10): 0890515093

Title: Guide to Creation Basics
Author: Institute for Creation Research
ISBN (10): 1935587153

Title: Ultimate Proof of Creation
Author: Dr. Jason Lisle
ISBN (10): 0890515689

Title: Beyond Intelligent Design
Author: Dr. Mel Mulder
ISBN (10): 1932205101

Title: A Line in the Sand: Defending Creation Truth
Author: Dr. Mel Mulder
ISBN (10): 159571961X

Title: The Genesis Record: A Scientific and Devotional Commentary on the Book of Beginnings
Author: Henry M. Morris III
ISBN (10): 0801072824

Title: God and Government: A Biblical, Historical, and Constitutional Perspective
Author: Gary DeMar
ISBN (10): 1936577038

Title: Assumptions that Affect Our Lives
Author: Christian Overman
ISBN (10): 0974342572

Title: Death in the City
Author: Francis A. Schaeffer
ISBN (10): 1581344023

Title: The Abolition of Man
Author: C.S. Lewis
ISBN (10): 0060652942

Title: Stop Worrying About Politics: (Start Serving Heaven)
Author: Dr. Fred Ray Lybrand
ISBN (10): 1494997509

Title: Christianity and Liberalism
Author: J. Gresham Machen
ISBN (10): 0802864996

Title: Things That Differ
Author: C.R. Stam
ISBN (10): 1893874257

Title: A Dispensational Theology
Author: Charles F. Baker
ISBN (10): 0898140269

Title: The Deliberate Dumbing Down of America, Revised and Abridged Edition
Author: Charlotte Thomson Iserbyt
ISBN (10): 0966707117

ONLINE RESOURCES:

The following website addresses currently (as of fall of 2014) provide excellent information of significant value to those interested in building a framework of logical thought based upon the truth of God and His Word (listed at random):

http://www.icr.org/
https://answersingenesis.org/ (https://answersingenesis.org/)
http://www.icr.org/
http://creationinthe21stcentury.com/
http://www.muldermel.com/
http://www.biblicalworldview.com/
http://www.fredraylybrand.com/
https://www.bereanbiblesociety.org/
http://deliberatedumbingdown.com/
http://c.shelfbloom.com/randolph/

Hands-on Opportunities:

Creation Museums (search online for other options in your local area):

http://creationmuseum.org/
http://7wonders.nwcreation.net/

Attend Biblical Worldview classes either online or on campus (search online for other options as well):

http://www.bereanbibleinstitute.org/

Bow the Knee (traditional)

There are moments on our journey following the Lord
Where God illumines ev'ry step we take.
There are times when circumstances make perfect sense to us,
As we try to understand each move He makes.
When the path grows dim and our questions have no answers,
turn to Him.

Bow the knee;
Trust the heart of your Father when the answer goes beyond what
you can see.
Bow the knee;
Lift your eyes toward heaven and believe the One who holds
eternity.
And when you don't understand the purpose of His plan,
In the presence of the King, bow the knee.

There are days when clouds surround us, and the rain begins to
fall,
The cold and lonely winds won't cease to blow.
And there seems to be no reason for the suffering we feel;
We are tempted to believe God does not know.
When the storms arise, don't forget we live by faith and not by
sight.

Let Everything Else Go (Phil Keaggy)

Chasing down hot air balloons on Sunday morning
In pace with a familiar tune I reach for nothing less but
something more
All the day and the wind is at my back most of the way, hey
yeah.

Holding conversation with a friend I know is near
Great anticipation fills my soul, it fills my heart, it fills the air
All the day and the wind is at my back ...

Oh, I can't wait to see you, Jesus, face to face
Nothing in this world can take Your place
All the pride of man laid low and all his works of gold
Nothing can compare with what You are
Let everything else go.

Let it all go.

And the wind is at my back ...

Oh, I can't wait to see you Jesus, face to face
Nothing in this world can take Your place
All the pride of man laid low and all his works of gold
Nothing can compare with what You are
Let everything else go.

Let it all go
Let everything else go.

The Orchestration of the Failure of Society

by

Jason Randolph

A seminal treatise regarding modern global society, the progression of technology and communication. Incorporating Biblical principles and concepts in opposition to the pursuits of humanism, post-modernism, existentialism, hedonism while illuminating the role of Satan in widely accepted social philosophies and sciences (as originally structured by the seven men discussed).

Demonstrates how the internet and other developing communication technologies, though not capable of being evil themselves, are being used to increase rebellion against that which is solely good, valuable and true.

w/ included annotated Humanist Manifestos

ISBN- 10: 0985682620
ISBN 13: 978-0-9856826-2-0

http://c.shelfbloom.com

www.ingramcontent.com/pod-product-compliance
Lightning Source LLC
Chambersburg PA
CBHW021342290326
41933CB00037B/425